MILESTONE MARGARITA

JASON YOUNG

Milestone Margarita

ISBN: 978-1-7359203-3-7

Copyright © 2020 by Jason Young

Published by Jason Young

Edited & Designed by Be Authentic Designs

DEDICATION

Taking something you wanted to do and making it
a reality. We were never made for boxes and they
can't take what they didn't give.
I'm up, I got this, I got us.

TABLE OF CONTENTS

5 INTRODUCTION

9 THE GAUNTLET

35 THE NATURAL STATE

61 BUT WAIT, THERE'S MORE

87 GOING BACK TO CALI

111 REALIZATION

129 CERTIFIED MAIL

141 PASSPORTS REQUIRED

149 TURBULENCE

159 HOLDING PATTERN

173 WHEELS DOWN

INTRODUCTION

I feel as if everything in life is about perspective. Everyone could physically lay eyes upon the same event and if you were to ask all in attendance to describe the event, you would have multiple and different descriptions of the same event as seen from multiple perspectives. Everyone witnessed the same event, yet each saw and interpreted it in a different perspective than their fellow event goers.

For me personally, I view life as a game, a game with levels one must complete successfully in order to proceed. You cannot access the next phase until you complete the current phase. You'll realize in life we seem to repeatedly fail the same tests and challenges. Therefore, if you would like to proceed to what lies ahead in the next level, you have to master your current level by conquering whatever it is holding you back.

You do that by getting real and ugly with yourself. Telling yourself the hard things you don't want to admit. The things that make you cringe when you're alone in complete silence and solitude. Deal with those things and watch things start to unfold. Before long, you'll look around and realize not only have you leveled up, but your surroundings have also changed.

Getting to this level in my life where I have this particular perspective has been a journey to say the least, one filled with more valleys than peaks, but those valleys were and still are part of the necessary challenges required in order for growth. That's some new soul-searching shit I recently picked up, but believe me when I say I wasn't always on this level. I basically want to share how I arrived at this point and some of the things I've encountered on this trip that have played a role in molding and shaping me into the man I am today.

Because this isn't an audio book, I'll do my best to help you feel the weight of my words since you can't hear the gravity of my voice.

I was established 1982 in Santa Maria, CA. I was born at Valley Community Hospital, lived off of N. Railroad, and grew up on Newlove. That's some Santa Barbara County version of "street credibility." I'm the youngest and coolest child, I may or may not have a low-key God complex at times, and I prefer solitude over people. Growing up, it was about being a kid, naps, and food. Everyone liked you, and there was no such thing as drama. The only thing we had to worry about was where we were going to hide when playing hide and go seek. Fast forward to high school, Freshman year of 1997, and those aforementioned luxuries would be nothing more than an afterthought. Up until this point in life, life had been a cake walk, and everything was sunshine and rainbows. This was the point in time where I was introduced to reality and began to understand how this game was played.

CHAPTER 1

○ ◉ ○ ○ ○

THE GAUNTLET

High school was something I was very much looking forward to because I could finally play football. Mom told me I wasn't allowed to play football until my freshman year because it would prevent my growth. There may or may not have been some truth to that, but I think it was because she didn't want to watch me possibly hurt myself.

Football wasn't the only reason I was looking forward to high school. I was growing up, able to drive, had more independence, making new friends etc. School for me had always been enjoyable for the most part, I never had any disciplinary issues, never struggled with academics, and was a great classmate to all students. So of course, my naive ass goes into high school expecting the same kind of treatment.

Well, that was definitely not the case. It may have been at times but overall, I found out very quickly that some people just will not like you. It doesn't matter what you do or say to them, in their minds you're their competition, enemy, or both.

A quick synopsis before going further. At the time, the town I grew up in was ethnically challenged. The diversity consisted of mostly Caucasian and Hispanic, peppered with some Black. When I say Black, I mean me, my sister, and our two black friends. We were about the only blemish of melanin in the area. Yes, there were more of us in town, but as far as this story is concerned, we were the Tuskegee Airmen of the 805.

Now, in order to get into this specific high school, one had to take an entrance exam, and based off of your scores you were categorized(labeled) and placed into one of three categories: High School Preparatory, College Preparatory, or Advanced classes.

Apparently, I was more of a low hanging fruit type because High School Preparatory, party of one, your table is ready. This was the first of many boxes I would be placed in, but it definitely wasn't the last. High School Prep classes were just a nice way of calling me remedial. In their eyes I was a one step above special needs students. Hell, a box of melted crayons had a brighter future than some of the kids I took classes with. Honestly, at the time I didn't think anything about my placement, nor did I care. I was in high school, I finally got to play football, and I only had three years left before I was free and clear of this legal obligation referred to as an education. So, in my eyes, I was all the way winning.

High School was a lot of firsts for me, and to say I wasn't ready would be a huge understatement. When school began it took a little getting used to because I now had seven periods and we would rotate those periods on different days. Instead of going to the same rotation of classes every day, we would rotate after our first break bell.

After our first two morning classes the bell would ring for break, and instead of going to third period after break, we would go to whichever class we were rotating that day and work our way back down. So, say we rotated six, we would go to first and second period, have break, go to sixth period, fifth, fourth, and finish the day with third. Sounds complicated but it really isn't too difficult to get accustomed to once you get in the swing of things. It was also the first time I started to feel uncomfortable around other people. Growing up I never had any issues making or sustaining friends, I was always a sponge, like Ariel. I wanted to learn and see everything, talk to strangers, ask questions, all of it.

I was so inquisitive as a child that my neighbor referred to me as Jason The Inquisitor. I had no idea what that meant when I was nine, but once I found out, I agreed he was pretty spot on. That inquisitive nature was still very much a part of me, but I was realizing I had to learn to reel it in because some of the people I was encountering were just as inquisitive about me as I was them. Thing is, neither of us seemed to have realized it at the time and what may have been innocent curiosity on both our behalves, quickly turned into disdain; at least on my end anyway. By the end of my time there I wouldn't have put them out if they were on fire. Not an exaggeration, just simply how I felt. In their only defense, I will say that I'm sure it was challenging for them to be encountering a six-foot two-inch freshman that didn't look or sound like any of them. When I say sound, I don't mean I failed to pronounce my words and mumbled like a zombie. I mean my voice was pretty deep for my age and I towered over most adults. From a physical standpoint I'm assuming I was both overwhelming and intimidating. At the time, these were traits I didn't necessarily wish to possess because they made it more difficult to get through high school due to the fact that I was perceived as a threat.

School was very much enjoyable for the most part. I had started two-a-day football practices two weeks prior to classes beginning, I was meeting and interacting with my new coaches, making what I thought were friends, and creating new memories. One morning after two-a-days, I was walking to the locker room when I was stopped by management. Management is what I'm going to refer to anyone who held disciplinary powers as. Powers that included but not limited to demerits, detention, suspension, and expulsion.

Before it's all said and done, I would be welcoming two of the previously mentioned four on the daily. Upon stopping me, it asked if my hair was going to be grown back out in time for the start of actual classes. To which I responded no, I highly doubt it. They responded by saying moving forward I needed to be more aware of the rule book in regard to the hair length required of all students. I thought that was weird, but I said okay and kept it moving. Now mind you, all I had done was cut my hair for Summer because who wants to be hot and wear a helmet with thick ass coarse hair while running around in the sun?

Not me, but hey, rules are rules, right? At the time I thought nothing of it, but it was just the first of many petty encounters with management.

Classes began and school really wasn't too challenging outside of the pace of things picking up a little. Literature was my favorite class mostly because my teacher was a complete nut but very passionate about what she was teaching. If you've ever taken Literature you know that some of those stories are a complete snooze fest, but if you can get creative with your method of teaching and sharing those stories, you may have a chance. Well, she definitely got creative. She would dress up and everything. Anything to engage her students and keep their attention. Looking back at it, it is definitely the effort and passion I respect because it was evident that not all teachers possessed this trait. Which brings me to my Math and Spanish tormentors. The Math guy was an old dinosaur that spent more time discussing his former job as a TSA agent than he did teaching mental abuse to humans that curriculums refer to as math. Maybe his method of the time he actually spent teaching worked for a handful of the students, but it definitely didn't work for me.

Needless to say I got left all the way behind in that class and had absolutely zero desire to catch up, and I must have blocked out all he said or attempted to teach because I couldn't tell you a single thing he said regarding math, but I could tell you all about his stories from his former job. Moving along to my Spanish captor, If I had to pick an absolute worst part of my day on a consistent basis while imprisoned at that institution, it would be anytime spent near or around this woman. The sound of her voice alone could replace water boarding as an interrogation technique. Now remember, I was in high school entry level Spanish. I learned more Spanish from the kids on my street than I ever did in that class. Actually learned a few words I would have enjoyed using on her, but, that's neither here nor there. Bottom line is she didn't like me, and I could not stand her.

Every day I had to deal with her "go to hell" glances which were greeted with my "you're still breathing?" stare. It was our form of hello. Needless to say, there was no love lost between the two of us, and once again I was just going nowhere fast regarding this amazing education I was supposed to be getting. I could speculate for days as to why we didn't get along, but I didn't care to find out and concluded she was a waste of both my time and effort. One particular day she sent me to management within the first two minutes of our session. This was bittersweet because I had seemed to get out of being tortured that day, but I was merely trading in one cell for another. I walked into class that morning, sat down, and the bell rang indicating it was time for torture to commence. Two minutes in and she's using her favorite torture device, her mouth! She's looking at me in the back of the classroom and tells me to leave. I'm sitting there grabbing my book while looking at her confused. I point to myself and shockingly ask her if she means me?

She assures me that she does in fact mean me as she violently throws her arm towards the door. I open my mouth to form the words, "I didn't do..." before she cuts me off and yells, "NOW!". Okay then, I'll just grab my things and be on my way. She calls management, informs them I'm in route, and that is where lucky me got to spend the rest of that period, learning absolutely nothing and swearing up and down I did nothing to merit this response. I was trying to explain class had just started and I was being asked to leave when I said or did nothing other than sit down. Once I realized it was futile to attempt further explanation of my perspective, it became more about counting down the minutes until I could leave and get to a class I actually enjoyed. Being stuck in that office smelling like loneliness, cats, and cigarettes was punishment enough.

Not all of the issues I experienced were handed down from my captors, some of the issues were created by my fellow captives, and since I wasn't your ideal target for bullying due to my size, kids had to get creative as to how they got under my skin. One of those ways was to ask things like, "Don't you have a test you should be failing?" Or by repeatedly asking where I placed in the school's advanced placement test. Anything they could do to remind me of my place. I was bigger than them but hey, make him feel small in his mind and we win. Maybe they didn't see what they were doing at the time, maybe they did, but I can tell you how it was received. If it wasn't the stupid jokes, it was dumb shit like having some seventeen-year-old rodeo reject throw a rope around my neck and rope me like cattle on the senior lawn in front of my classmates. You want to talk about embarrassing, this was it. One thing I can't stand is to be embarrassed, and this asshole just had the misfortune of not only embarrassing me, but also completely shitting on my race. I'm guessing his stupid ass was too ignorant to understand the stain slavery has implemented on this country, or maybe he was so entitled he failed to give a single fuck prior to roping a black male like a fucking animal.

He quickly realized the errors of his ways and tried apologizing, needless to say I told him to shove both that apology and rope up his inbred ass, and to stay the entire fuck away from me. Best part about all of this is how absolutely nothing came from this and he went on about his business as if nothing happened. This was an instance had the roles been reversed I would have been suspended or expelled for placing a rope around one's neck and constricting their airway. This asshole cut off my oxygen supply and didn't get so much as a slap on the wrist. Had this taken place anywhere outside of that school's property I would like to say it would be attempted murder charges, who knows, either way, that was the first time I realized white kids were playing life by a different set of rules, and it was evident I wasn't going to be able to get through a day of school without encountering some form of bullshit. Once that became abundantly clear, I started expecting it, it made the days somewhat easier to deal with.

One of the most difficult things to deal with was when things management began saying I did started to involve parents that volunteered at the school, parents that knew my parents, parents that would more than likely bring it to my parent's attention. The last thing I needed was for my parents to be hearing speculation as to what their son was doing wrong at school. Mom and dad didn't subscribe to the third-party information line, and if we knew we had done something wrong they better hear it from us first. That's just it though, I didn't do anything wrong. A particular instance of this was when one day, our teacher had us playing shirts and skins football for our physical education period. I was placed on skins and obviously had to remove my shirt. On the way back to the locker room, we have to pass an office that some volunteers (parents) work in during the day to help with school projects. I'm now in the locker room changing and preparing to head to lunch and as I'm walking out I hear my name being called to the office over the intercom. It wasn't the fact that I was being summoned, it was the tone associated with the voice and the looks from other classmates as I walked to the office. As I would soon find out, that was the third time I had been called, but for whatever reason, I failed to hear. Upon entering the office there was a line; as there usually was during lunch because all the teachers had turned in their snitch lists, and captives were lining up for punishment. So, I did what any normal captive would do and got in the back of the line because who wants to be first to receive punishment? That was short lived because apparently, they had grown tired of waiting on me. My football coach who doubled as my P.E. teacher sticks his head out of the office, looks into the back of the line, and motions me into the office. The students in line were looking at me with such relief because apparently, I had just volunteered as tribute, and was about to be the sacrificial black for all their daily sins. I hesitantly walked to the front, walked into the office, and was told matter of factly to sit down. I sat down and asked what it is I did that would require such an aggressive response on their behalf? They both look at me like disappointed parents and my coach asked:

"You think showing people your ass is funny?"
To which I responded by laughing and asking,
"WHAT,? What are you talking about? Have you
met my parents? Show my ass?" When I
stopped laughing, I told them I had absolutely
no idea what they were talking about and I
would never in the history of ever show my ass
in such an environment. I followed up by
explaining I was more terrified of what my dad
would do If I even formed the thought of doing
something so outlandish, and you summoning
me shows just how little you know about me.
They failed to realize I was taught the children
are a reflection of their parents, therefore, me
doing something that would bring unwanted
attention and embarrassment to not only me,
but my entire family as well, was something I
would never contemplate. They proceeded to
tell me some of the mothers working in the
office that day were highly offended. I
responded, "As they should be, but not with me
because it wasn't me." I still to this day have no
idea who in the hell showed one of those ladies
their ass, or if it even happened for that matter.

Nor do I know who they mistook for me because mine was definitely the only black ass in line that day. I guess all is well that ends well, but at this point getting sent to management for random off the wall shit was becoming a hemorrhoid.

For all the shit that went on in high school, there were some good moments with a handful of people that I wouldn't trade for the world. They are a part of some of my fondest memories, and at the time provided a much needed break from the monotony of getting my ass kicked Monday through Friday, 7:45am to 2:45pm. Some more heartfelt moments were the bonding that was made during track season, the basketball tournament road trips, and the basketball practices that were more challenging than track practice. How does that even happen? How were we running more in basketball practice than we did at track practice?

Because our coach was a firm believer in being the best conditioned team on the court, especially in the fourth quarter. Some days our practices would begin on the track before we even stepped foot on the court. If we weren't hustling hard enough or we slacked on help defense, we heard about it in the form of wind sprints and quarter mile laps. This was standard operating procedure on how to make teenagers hate you, but apparently he knew what he was doing because it created a bond and understanding between teammates. Those bonds were also prevalent throughout our track team, probably more so for track events because parents drove personal vehicles and we would carpool. We referred to ourselves as trackbebes, and yes, I'm aware of the spelling, but we were different, so it worked, and if you replace the T with a C it would paint a very accurate picture of our group.

Our track coach who doubled as my study hall teacher was more like a liaison between me and management. He understood and saw me for me. He wasn't intimidated by my stature, wasn't afraid to approach me, and spoke to me like he gave a shit, not like he hated me. He was a little weird, had no concept of personal space, and the man would literally take a candy bar out of my hand while I'm eating it, take a bite, then hand it back to me. That's just how he was., He coached us hard on the track, but treated us with respect. I've lived by Maya Angelou's concept, "You will never forget how someone made you feel," and in reference to this particular life event, I have the memory of an elephant.

My mom, God bless her, this woman was always ready to fight on my behalf, and she was always at that school trying to actively paint the picture of who her son really was. Telling them they had no idea what they were talking about, and they have made it to where I no longer want to attend school. It was great seeing and knowing mom had my back like that, but it was okay because me gone is ultimately what they wanted, and it was reciprocated on my end. They had established which kids were worth putting time and effort into, and I definitely wasn't in that group. The lengths to which they would reach to get rid of me were astronomical, I was once summoned to the office for speeding in the parking lot. Now mind you I drove a 1998 Nissan Pathfinder and this parking lot had speed bumps every ten feet. A big square lot with multiple speed bumps, yet somehow, I found a way to speed and endanger other students? I don't think you understand the concept here, I go out of my way to avoid being placed anywhere on your radar and will walk around the building just to avoid making eye contact with you fucks, yet you think I really want to speed and give you a reason to confront me? I was the one in High School Preparatory classes, yet I'm convinced they were the dumb ones, common sense really wasn't so common amongst management. Was really a case of the blind leading the blind regarding how to deal with me, and the two that did have a rapport with me were outnumbered two to whatever the fuck, two to all the rest, how about that? We'll just say the ones that wanted me gone far outweighed the ones that wanted me to stay. This school was a fucking joke, I wasn't wanted anywhere, and I was too stupid to see it, my teammates didn't even give a shit about me. Never voted captain even though I accounted for over half of the offense and special teams. Attend the end of the year banquets to have the coaches stand and rave about you, your talents, say that if it weren't for me our team wouldn't be where we were, followed by saying these awards were voted on by the players. Then proceed to give every high-profile award to everyone except me. Began the ceremony singing my praises and ended with giving me a participation certificate. This was what my teammates thought of me? That was the night I said fuck that school and fuck these people. My dad actually had to calm me down that night. He came into my room and told me man can't promote me. He said my promotions come from God. He wasn't wrong, but in my mind, it was still to hell with these people. I'm done with them, they can all kiss my ass, and moving forward, that was my mindset.

Junior year my mom had asked for a meeting with my counselors and teachers and asked each of them where they saw me in five years. Their responses were mostly what we expected; dropped out of high school, nowhere, basically a fucking loser incapable of doing anything other than dribbling or catching a ball, running faster, or jumping higher than the other kids. For whatever reason I was nothing more than a problem they wanted to rid themselves of. They told mom I wasn't like my sister, and that I didn't have the focus or drive to succeed. When my mom asked my English teacher what she thought of me, she was the only one who said I have plenty of potential and went out of her way to point out things she saw as strengths. The takeaway from that meeting was a resonating clarification as to my future at that school, lines were drawn, and sides were unveiled. You don't want me here, so why not become the asshole teenager you already believe I am? I no longer gave a single fuck about anything educational, and I definitely wasn't going to make the remainder of my time at that shit hole pleasant for them. I quit the football team before they could dismiss me for grades and didn't even bother with basketball.

In reference to sports, this was the first time I wasn't actively playing organized sports since second grade, and when I told my football coach I was quitting, he told me there was no future for me in basketball. In my mind I was laughing cause he failed to realize it wasn't about choosing basketball over football, I no longer have a future at this school and I'm just taking what little control I feel like I have left. This isn't about one sport or the other, this was about my time at that school coming to an end. I knew my Junior year would be my last at this place and It couldn't come fast enough. I was now on academic probation and had mustered a one point go fuck yourself GPA which gave them exactly what they needed to permanently dismiss me. School had been out for a day when the house phone rang. When I answered, I recognized the voice; it was satan. It asked if my parents were home to which I answered no.

It then proceeded to say it believed I knew what this phone call was regarding and informed me of it's and their decision to expel me for repeated failure to meet academic standards or some shit. Basically, a fancy way of saying I failed to maintain the grades required to attend their prestigious educational facility. I said cool and it asked if I could have my parents return its phone call. I hung up while it was talking, and that was that, no need to drag this on. Rip the band aid off and go our separate ways; definitely no love lost. I say that now, but at that time I was very upset. I was seventeen, had no idea what was next for me, still had a year left of high school, was angry at everyone, couldn't get into the school I wanted to go to for zoning reasons, and the school in my district wasn't anyone's first choice education wise. If you were wanting to get into some shit other than educational, this would be the school you'd attend. To clarify, in this instance "shit other than educational" means, gang violence, sex, and plenty of drugs.

I'm aware most high schools have these issues, but those issues ran in abundance at this particular cesspool, and needless to say I definitely wasn't going there, not with the attitude and outlook I had on the world. Thankfully my parents being the all wise wizards they were, recognized the potential for severe disaster, informed me I was moving to Arkansas, and that I would be living with my aunt and uncle. There I was, seventeen-year-old me being told I was leaving Santa Barbara County, California and trading it in for Craighead County Arkansas. I was flabbergasted and appalled, I mean, the AUDACITY!

Honestly though, it wasn't like I was leaving much behind other than a few close friends and some visual scenery I'd later on realize I took for granted. I had a girlfriend, but it wasn't like we were ever in love or anything. She tolerated me and I'm pretty sure her dad hated me which was only more of a reason for me to leave. There was no longer anything there for me. The time at that place in my life had come to an end, and I was having a hard time. My entire situation was up in the air and I had little to no control over the process. I was trading in oceans and palm trees for humidity and mosquitoes, neither of which anyone in their right mind would be happy about. The average temperature where I grew up was around a low of 34 and a high of possibly 90. Where I was going, the temperature ranged from 5 degrees or lower, to highs of triple digit hell. Ice was common and snow was a thing. I would be needing an entirely new wardrobe and I was going to have to get accustomed to not only weather and environmental conditions, but also with people and their narrow-minded thinking.

Change is never easy and when you're only a teenager experiencing something like this, it seems like the whole world is crashing down on you. The teenage version of me definitely couldn't see any light at the end of the proverbial tunnel, and when I was fortunate enough to see even a glimpse of light, it mimicked more of a train and less the end of a shitty journey.

CHAPTER 2

○ ◉ ○ ○ ○

THE NATURAL STATE

July of 2000 marked the beginning of my new adventure. I was settled in my new place and preparing to start two-a-days football practice. This was my first introduction to my new harsh reality, and it wasn't going to be like practice in Santa Barbara County. There would be no cool temperatures, brisk winds, or gentle fog during morning practice, and there definitely wouldn't be any Santa Ana winds occasionally blowing through to cool you off during the second practice. This was a start off tough and only gets tougher ordeal. You adapted or you didn't, either way, the hits kept on coming. It took me one week of practice before I felt fully adjusted to the humidity. I had to learn to hydrate more and make better food choices if I wanted to make it through practice. In the first week I lost ten pounds, and during conditioning periods my coach would yell out:

"Hot enough for you Cali?" Actually, yes, it is, thank you very much. For the first time in two years I was having fun. I was enjoying something for a change, I was playing a new position in football and enjoying it immensely. I had finally grown into my body and was now 6'5 260 pounds and ran a 4.5 forty-yard dash. These attributes made me an ideal candidate for defensive line, so you can imagine my satisfaction when I was placed on the defensive line! My new position coach would always say he wished he had me for four years because though I had the size, I was still very raw at the position. Prior to moving I was just tall, lanky, and fast, over six feet, only weighed 175 pounds, and played offense and special teams. Now I'm learning a new position and doing the hitting instead of receiving the hits.

Football afforded me the opportunity to establish some form of connection with my new teammates. It was a little challenging in the sense that I was the new kid, and of course everyone wants to test the new kid.

There were moments where the occasional letting off of testosterone occurred but nothing that ever got completely out of hand. Just the way things go when a new person is inserted into a locker room. I was being thrown into their lives and they wanted to see what I was about. Coming from what I just left in California, a part of me was still in my fuck you mindset, so this could have easily ended before it even began for me in Arkansas. However, as my mom would say: "By the grace of God." Off the field I just wanted to go to class and home. I wasn't interested in going out of my way to make friends, and I definitely wasn't looking for a girlfriend. Somehow, I ended up with both in the form of one with Shannon, and that was perfect because I'm all about some two for one type shit.

Prior to being cast into this sea of newness, my dad told me to be careful when dating because things in the South were and are different then I was accustomed to. I responded by telling him I was well aware of the South's sheet and horse perspective on interracial dating, I would do my best not to offend anyone's fragile sensibilities, and I would do this all while steering clear of any tiki torch rallies. It was a new path of racism to navigate, but hey, such is life, I got this. Which brings me back to the aforementioned two for one. Shannon not only knew my cousins prior to my arrival but one of her friends was actually dating my cousin at the time, and when she found out I was moving there to attend school, she went all Nancy Drew, and set her sights on yours truly.

While heading to practice one day I was walking through the commons area when I saw Shannon standing with her friend. She was holding a fountain drink and when I asked her where mine was, I received a shy "I don't know," accompanied by a smile which is obviously what one hopes for when shooting their shot. That smile led to us talking more consistently and eventually dating. We went to the Back To School dance separately because I was still unsure of where I stood with her parents, and didn't want to pick her up at her house because I couldn't be sure my doing so wasn't going to recreate a scene from Mississippi Burning. We linked up at the dance, mostly talked, and began getting to know each other. Followed the dance with a midnight date to Waffle House, and this was the night you could say we officially started dating.

Our first real date was a trip to the movies where I picked her up from her friend's house, so she didn't get in trouble for going out with me. That didn't work because snitches see everything, and her mother grounded her for being seen at the movies with "that black guy." It's laughable now, but at the time it was pretty fucking annoying and was almost the last straw for me. When she told me she was grounded for being seen in public with me, it pissed me off. To think someone was losing their freedom simply because they were seen with me. Shit was offensive and I had to take a moment and ask myself if this relationship was worth pursuing. My thinking was this is straight up bullshit. Here I am with enough on my plate as it is, and now the woman I'm interested in is being grounded because I'm black and she's white. The year was 2000 and we were still having that fucking conversation.

Shannon was persistent though; she didn't allow her being grounded to keep her from talking to me. I thought she was crazy! She would tell me to come over and I would colorfully decline until I knew her parents weren't going to lose their shit if I were to be seen there. We all know how stand your ground laws work in the South, and I wasn't about to be on anyone's Ten O'clock news misrepresented as a suspect in a home invasion. I told her if she wanted to see me, she could continue coming over to my uncle's or my place once my parents arrived. Not to say I wouldn't go to her house, but it was for short amounts of time and usually while her parents were gone because at that point, I still hadn't officially met my in-laws yet which made us even because she hadn't formally met my parents at that time either. She had spoken to my dad on the phone, but she wouldn't meet him face to face until October of that year.

November arrived, my parents have now been settled into Jonesboro for a month, and now that Shannon had formally met them, the time was nearing when I would be reciprocating. To say this was nerve wracking and one of the hardest things I ever had to do would be an understatement. Not because I knew at the time she was going to be my future mother-in-law, but because I was black, she had already grounded Shannon, I was dealing with really bad allergies, my eyes were bloodshot, and the eerie stigma of racism loomed over that town like a rain cloud. It was now winter in Jonesboro, the Winter Formal school dance was nearing, and this would be the reason I was afforded the lovely opportunity to formally meet my future in-laws. When the time came, prior to walking in all I could focus on was how bad my eyes looked and how she was going to think I just smoked an entire bag of weed.

I walked into the living room and my future

mother-in-law was sitting on the couch staring at me like a disapproving parent. I don't remember what was said, but I know I formed complete sentences and used manners, and that's all I remember other than trying to get the fuck out of that house as fast as possible. I also don't recall what I said to my father-in-law, or if he was even there. All I remember was the way she looked at me, and how it made me feel. That was the second night I contemplated if I really wanted to pursue or deal with any of this. Luckily for me I have all this charm and once I put Ma's mind at ease it was smooth sailing. I just had to convince her I was the right kind of black which is cool because she needed to convince me she was the right kind of white. This was definitely a mutual feeling and both parties involved needed to convince the other that their intentions were pure. When we finally understood each other and I was coming around for dinners all the time, she did a complete 180. She was asking me what I liked for dinner, I'm sorry, supper. I was also learning that in the South lunch is dinner and dinner is supper.

She wanted to know about my past, met my parents, the whole nine. This was weird at first because she was being nice to me, and If you know anything about black people, we are a little cautious of white people when they start being nice to us, especially when it's a sudden change. Though things were definitely better between us on that front, I never missed an opportunity to be an ass for having to endure her shit. One night we were headed to eat fish at this hole in the wall restaurant in the middle of nowhere. On our way there we drove past an open field that had this huge tree in the middle.

This tree looked as if it had been there for years, like it had endured slavery years. I sat up in my seat and said look Myra, that's where your people used to hang my ancestors. She scoffed, turned around in her seat and said: "JASON!" Had she known my middle name at the time I'm sure she would've used it. I laughed and left it at that, but now she definitely knew I'm petty as hell, so get ready because this is the first of many petty moments I have reserved for you.

I was definitely dragging that shit out, but it's all part of my charm and I'm a package deal, so, the good with the great.

Now that we had established this lovely banter, I'd come over daily after school and stay for hours. I'd come over on the weekends just to hang out and if we weren't there, we were at my house. This was wash and repeat behavior once football ended because I didn't play basketball or run track my senior year. I had nothing but time on my hands in a place with very little to do, and when I say very little to do, I mean if you didn't duck hunt, you were watching tv or asleep. The Bible Belt also has this ordinance shit referred to as a dry county, which meant the sale of alcohol was prohibited within county lines and if you wanted to get sauced you had to drive to butt fuck nowhere until you're eventually far enough outside of county jurisdiction. At which point you'd see an alcohol surplus store equipped with its own drive through and menu of best sellers. This was all new to me because I was accustomed to walking into any store or gas station and seeing various alcoholic beverages. Things were definitely different here, and I was learning in and outside of school.

School was going well other than the occasional dip shits you'd have to deal with, faculty included. There was this particular older troll who always went out of her way to make sure I wasn't hugging or holding hands with Shannon. She would ask if that hug was worth detention and asked in a manner which suggested detention scared me or something, like I wasn't just expelled from my last place of educational residency. Yes, this hug is absolutely worth detention because it's the best part of my day, so feel free to put me in detention you trifling heifer. The remainder of the school year went off without any significant issues other than my fat ass almost not fitting into my slacks. For two weeks leading up to graduation my mom had told me to try on these slacks she had bought for graduation. She kept saying try them on so I can take them back in time if they don't fit. Graduation night arrived, I still hadn't tried them on, and guess what, they didn't fit and now I was having a tantrum hopping, pulling, swearing, and tugging trying to fit my ass in my slacks. All the while my best friend Justin is laughing, Shannon is trying not to laugh while telling me to suck it in, my sisters are looking at me like they're not surprised, and my dad was off getting ready while mom was doing her best not to kill me. This was happening an hour before graduation and we were running out of options until we settled on a safety pin and called it a night. I graduated with a 3.2 leading one to the conclusion the change of scenery actually worked. Who would have thought? That's why I was the child in this story and not the adult.

Now that I had graduated, I had little to no idea what I wanted to do but knew I didn't want to do any of it in Jonesboro. I wasn't too fond with the idea of pursuing a higher education and was even less fond with the idea of having to apply. My dad had suggested the military, but you could say I wasn't mature enough to hear that as a plausible idea at the time. If you remember history, that was around the time we invaded Iraq and that was all I could think about. I was never worried about basic training; I was concerned with the high possibility of deployment to a combat zone at 18. It wasn't necessarily ranking very high on my list. Even still, it would have still been a better option than college. Somehow, they let me sneak into college, and me barely getting in was equal to the effort in which I put forth during my short tenure at this institution of higher learning. Once I was in, I realized I still hated school, thought most of the shit was pointless, never felt like I fit, and I'd rather watch paint dry than have to sit through anyone's lectures. To me, college felt like having to sit through a church sermon, and not just any sermon, but a Southern Black Baptist sermon. If you've never had the misfortune, picture if you will. Old wooden pews, no air conditioning, a pastor who not only yells and repeats himself, but also swears nobody hears him. Elderly persons flabbergasted by how much you've grown, the stench of dust and moth balls, cough syrup, old lady perfume, and voila, picturesque! Felt like I was walking their path instead of finding my own. For me college was a formality I should have skipped instead of wasting a year of my life trying to fit in where I never belonged. A lot of questioning and more uncertainty is all college ever provided me. I lasted a full year before leaving, and the college experience was over before it even started. I had a few memorable moments during my brief stint, but the idea of school and a piece of paper determining my worth, they could keep that bullshit.

Upon leaving college I moved in with my sister, started working for UPS, and eventually bought a 1996 Impala SS. If you know even a little about cars, you know this is a pretty badass vehicle, this one in particular had chameleon paint compiled of five colors depending on your current view of the vehicle. As flashy as it was though, it wasn't very practical for winters in Northwest Arkansas. I ended up selling it and buying my more practical truck. This was around the same time I switched jobs and left UPS to begin working with at risk youth. I was assigned to a facility that was divided into two sides, one side focused on behavioral issues, and the other on drug use.

Working with these young men was an experience because I formed small connections and realized I'm impacting how they're going to view men that become authoritative figures in their future lives. Most of the youth didn't have viable father figures to begin with, and the ones that did wouldn't necessarily classify theirs as viable. That thought was always in the back of my mind and when dealing with them I'd tell myself I had to be stern, mean what I say, be unwavering, and never forget where to draw the line. I could be their friend but establish and make them understand I was in fact, not their friend. I also had to always take the temperature in the room because we all know how adolescence and testosterone mix; and as employees we wanted to avoid any volatile situations because the training rules required we bear hug these kids if and when they're raging pissed. I understand rules and all, but I can tell you right now, I knew the background of those kids. I've heard them tell their little stories in passing, and if you think for a second I wouldn't fight one should they come at me, I'd categorize you as stupid.

Outside of work, Shannon and I had just bought our first home, she had just begun working as an RN, and we were expecting our first child. This was the first time in a long while things actually felt somewhat normal, like I finally found some sort of solid foundation to build upon. I say that because prior to working with these kids, buying a house, and getting pregnant, there was a period where I was severely depressed, nothing in my life was going close to any direction I wanted it to, I wasn't sleeping, and I had blown up to 360 pounds, saying I had a problem is an understatement. Food was my best friend, especially fast food. Hell, those poor diet choices definitely contributed to my Crohn's

Disease, and when I look back at the timeline it fits perfectly. I was easily eating enough food to feed four adults, had no form of physical exercise, and couldn't care less about my health, a diet only raccoons would be jealous of.

Back at work I was building a slight rapport with a few of the kids. I was beginning to see them as individuals and not just troubled youth. We would go back and forth while still trying to maintain that line of mutual respect. One day I was working the behavior side and there was this kid, for privacy reasons I'll refer to him as J. J was maybe five feet tall, the only white kid on that side, and it was clear he was very comfortable around minorities. So much so, there was no way you could convince him he was white. We used to call him Paul Wall. If you don't know who that is, I suggest your preferred search engine. On this particular day we were getting them ready for down time and J wasn't trying to hear any of it. He was pacing back and forth rapping lyrics to a song he had been writing in his journal while ignoring the hell out of us.

When we finally got his attention, he responded by calling me a MWT, and before I could ask him what the fuck an MWT was, this little shit said a man with titties. That was it, I was done with this disrespectful fuck. When I stood up, he walked into his room laughing and getting fist bumps from his fellow minions. He got his shot in, but he ultimately ended up where I wanted him, and I didn't write him up for it because it was original and made me laugh. Hurt a little, but the truth usually does, and we all know kids are brutally honest. He also wasn't necessarily wrong because I was still shedding that 360-pound frame so I'm sure I did look like I needed to wear a bra at some point. It was what it was, filed it under motivation and kept it moving.

Back home we were getting closer to being married and preparing for the arrival of our daughter, and since neither of us had the desire nor funds to have an extravagant wedding at the time, it was the quick and easy route for us, courthouse party of two. Quick and easy with no debt, perfect! Nothing over the top about it; it was during the middle of the week, we met at the courthouse after we got off work, had some random witness, said our I do's, and went home. I think we ordered pizza. Nothing about how marriage unfolded for us was normal. My proposal came in the car ride home from the dentist. We were having a random life conversation, I was staring out the window, looked at her and said let's just get married. She looked at me like I was crazy for a few seconds, said okay, and that was that, 22-year-old logic isn't very logical at all.

Now that we were married, expecting, and living in our first home, we thought things were going great, well they were going great until I was let go from my job for almost kicking a kid's ass. I'll admit I lost my shit, and could have handled it better, but I never laid hands on the kid, and I told the staff someone needed to check his ass, followed by a few choice words about how they baby these young men and all that bear hugging shit was trash. They weren't wrong for letting me go, I'm just sorry it unfolded the way it did. Watching it all on film while sitting in front of a disciplinary board was like watching film study the next day when you're the one that lost the game for the team. It was a pretty shitty moment and I'm glad it was a video with no audio because we all have peaks and valleys, and this was definitely one of my valleys. Now instead of two incomes, we had only one. Thankfully for us, the cost of living in Arkansas wasn't very high, plus I could stay home and raise our daughter. Yes, I was actually looking forward to that, which tells you how naïve I was. I had no idea how to raise a child, especially a baby girl. I was terminated from my job in January of 06 and our daughter was born in March of the same year. Once our daughter Sierra arrived, it was hit the ground running. Everything was all good when you're at the hospital, but like I told the doctor and nurses, you can buy a vehicle and it comes with warranties, free oil changes, and tire rotations for either an extended amount of time or life. However, when you have a baby and leave the hospital, it's good luck, hope you make it, you're on your own, Godspeed. Shannon was only on maternity leave for 6 weeks, so this gave me ample opportunities to log fatherhood hours.

For the first few weeks I was treating Sierra like glass, I would hold her like she was my source of oxygen and sometimes placed my finger under her nostrils to make sure she was still breathing. During this phase there wasn't much sleeping involved on my end because I was worried something would happen to her. She was an amazing sleeper; we'd put her in bed around 8pm and she wouldn't wake up until 9am the next morning. We learned early on to never wake a sleeping baby, so she slept until she woke up on her own. Leading me to eventually realize I better sleep while I can and not worry about her when she's actually sleeping. You spend half the day trying to get them to sleep, and here I am stressing because she was asleep. I was doing this parenting shit all wrong, but Sierra and I were in the same boat because I too had to learn to crawl before I could walk. To say it was challenging would be an understatement. There were days Sierra couldn't be consoled, didn't want to be touched, wasn't taking her bottle, didn't want in her swing, and wouldn't sleep to save her life. That would all be okay if she weren't screaming fuck you in baby language the entire day. The day she did this, I was ready to call it quits. I had exhausted all plausible options until I tried one last thing; I laid a pile of blankets in the walk-in closet floor, turned on the accent light in the bathroom, surrounded her in a wall of pillows, cracked the closet door, and left. When I went back to check on her five to ten minutes later, she was asleep, success! Sometimes you just have to get creative. Poor child was so sleepy she couldn't stand it. She was teaching me so many things just as I was her. I had to learn to understand her and she had to learn how to communicate with me. Mastering this process allowed me to distinguish what her different cries meant. It was like me translating her screams when Shannon would ask what was wrong with her. I'd say her stomach hurts, give her to me, I'd burp her, and she'd smile. Shannon would roll her eyes and I'd say don't hate because I nail this dad shit. Parenting was slowly coming together for me and it wasn't as bad as I had originally thought; challenging at times yes, but such is life.

This was learn as you go, just like I learned to never place the car seat on the hood of the car. One evening we were getting ready to leave and I had just placed Sierra in her car seat. I had her strapped in and sat her on the hood of the Yukon while I opened the car door. I thought I had placed her far enough towards the front window that she wouldn't move or slide, however, when I went to open the car door, the vibrations sent the car seat shooting down the hood of the car towards the ground. I tried to grab her and missed. My heart dropped thinking I had just dropped my baby on her face!

I run around to the front and the car seat handle had acted as a kick stand catching the car seat and propping it up. Since she was securely fastened in her seat prior to her trip, she was good. When I went to grab her seat, she was smiling like she enjoyed it while I was trying to catch my breath, but as I said, learn as you go. Speaking of which, we also learned living with one income was manageable for a few years until it wasn't. Building new schools meant increased taxes and us being the young, dumb, and extremely naïve first-time home buyers, we didn't lock in a fixed mortgage rate which allowed it to increase, and we got behind on our mortgage. As you all know, banks frown upon this behavior and we needed a plan, I needed a job, a career actually, and I needed it yesterday. We formulated the plan of us listing the house for sale and moving to Missouri to be close to family. Shannon would begin work at a great hospital, and I would begin classes that August at the local police academy. After a year of open houses and no offers, it became clear selling the house would be a box that remained unchecked, and because we literally couldn't afford to sit around and wait any longer, we chose to file bankruptcy, surrender the house, and began our new life.

○ ● ○ ○ ○

CHAPTER 3

BUT WAIT, THERE'S MORE

N ow that we had completed the move to Missouri, the plan was to graduate the academy, get hired on at a department, and finally begin my career in law enforcement; or so I thought. To say those plans went to shit would be an understatement.

Our move to Missouri marked the first time Sierra would be attending pre-school and becoming socialized with other children. Prior to moving, she had been to a few programs in order to get acclimated to being around other people and children, but nothing as consistent as this would be. This was also challenging for me because I don't like other people watching my children and the thought of leaving her with complete strangers for hours throughout the day scared me. As I said, she had only been to a few programs, wasn't fond of most people, and only took naps when I laid down with her. I knew I had to eventually accept it and know she'd be okay, but it didn't make it any easier when the moment arrived.

Her first day arrived and as you can guess, she screamed in everyone's face, didn't want to be bothered or touched, and ran after us when we tried to leave. It wasn't pretty, may have mimicked a kidnapping training video at times but we got through it. Every drop off became easier, eventually reached a point where screaming was no longer involved, and she would actually wave good-bye without crying. Reaching that point was an obvious milestone because it was now one less thing I had to worry about and could focus my attention and efforts on school.

The Academy wasn't as difficult as I had made it out to be in my mind. A few weeks before actual classes began, we had orientation. At this orientation there were a plethora of law enforcement agencies and they're telling us what we can expect from them, what they expect from us, blah, blah, blah. While I'm sitting there, I'm looking around the room, listening to them speak, and thinking this is all a little overwhelming. From that point on I had made it more difficult for myself than I should have. I should have just went in with no expectations instead of driving myself crazy with all the possible scenarios and outcomes. In my mind I had made this out to be some unachievable, insurmountable event, when in reality it was challenging at times, yes, but definitely not impossible. The hardest thing to adjust to, was PT (Physical Training). I wasn't completely out of shape, but I wasn't necessarily in shape either. That lasted all of two weeks; two weeks of road runs, bear crawls, frog hops, lunges, pushups, wheelbarrows, and all kinds of other creative muscle memory exercises was all it took to get my not necessarily in shape ass all the way in shape. I remember drawing a line through my instructor's name and replacing it with the word SATAN. I despised the man for all the wrong reasons, but in the end, he was the reason I adjusted so quickly. During PT he would push me to keep going when I wanted to quit, and also found ways to encourage while at the same time distract me from the pain. It was definitely a love hate thing on my end, but growth is uncomfortable, and iron can only be sharpened by iron.

Inside the classroom I was once again the only blemish of color. I was accustomed to being the only black person, this was nothing new but what bothered me was that it was 2008 and people still didn't feel comfortable around me. Whenever our instructors would tell stories involving any one of color, they would start to sweat and trip over their words while looking at me, like they were going to offend me by saying the suspect was black. It was a little funny at times, but others it seemed slightly sad because it further displayed our deficiencies as humans and spotlighted ignorance we can only pray to one day move on from.

Throughout the academy we would be called

into the main office to meet with the director. He would ask us how we thought we were doing, then follow that with how we were actually doing in our training. Step it up a notch or we should continue as is, basically an evaluation you would receive at any place of employment. This was the first time I was told I should apply at a park, they seriously looked me in my face and told me the parks and recreation department would be a good fit for me. I honestly don't know how they expected me to take some dumb shit like that, but he said it in a way in which he expected me to be excited about it. Like I'm waking up every day dealing with satan and questioning if I want to continue all of it for the possibility of working in a fucking park? Inside I wanted to tell him to shove that entire idea up his crinkly, gentrified ass, but instead I smiled, said thank you for the information, and left. Meanwhile my classmates are discussing their evaluations and its recommendations for this department, or I know a guy, let me see what I can do. I quickly realized it had little to do with my effort, and more to do with being black. Apparently, I was only fit to cite people for littering and feeding the ducks after hours. Even still, I believed these were odds I'd eventually overcome and end up where I envisioned myself; and though that may have been the belief, it definitely wasn't the case.

I went on to graduate in December of 2008 with a POST A License, which meant I had met the Police Officer's Standard of Training to become a Police Officer in the states of both Missouri and Kansas, and that certification was valid five years from the date of reception. Equating to me having until December 2013 to secure a job in law enforcement before I would have to repeat the academy again in order to obtain recertification. Now that I had graduated, the hard work was behind me, or so I was naïve enough to believe. I was not sponsored coming into the academy, meaning I didn't have a job offer with a department waiting for me contingent upon successful completion of the academy. Only two cadets in our class were sponsored coming in and the rest of us had to apply and go through the rigorous and mundane process of filling out PHQ's; which is short for Personal History Questionnaire. These questionnaires were the most time-consuming part of the application process because they require everything about you. Some departments were more in depth than others, but for the most part they all wanted to know each place of residency I held throughout the previous ten years, along with any roommates, neighbors, bosses, and co-workers to the best of my recollection. Some wished to go as far back as your first-grade teacher while others wanted your credit and drug use history followed by how many times you've used. A ton of paperwork for the possibility of a call back, to maybe be assigned a written test date, which hopefully leads to an interview. For the first two years it was a lot of excitement followed by constant disappointment, and after submitting so many applications and going to the mailbox daily in hopes of some good news only to receive a letter saying they've chosen another candidate. It became hard to continue believing things would turn around for me.

I began believing I would never become anything more than what others said I would be, never have anything I wanted, and assumed I was destined to go nowhere fast even when I had what I thought was a good plan. However, feeling sorry for one's self only lasts so long before life reminds you, you're still alive, you're expecting your second child, and you have no time to cry about problems you can't solve. I still had three years left to land a job in law enforcement, so it wasn't the end of the road here, merely a slight detour.

While I was waiting to hear back from departments, I needed to do something, I had to work. With that in mind, while still applying at departments, I started working in the delivery department for a furniture company in Olathe, Kansas. This afforded me the luxury of being able to get out of the house every day, have a routine, and feel like I was contributing in some way to my family. The job was fun until it wasn't. It wasn't something or anything I wanted to do long term, and the man I was usually partnered with was a bum to say the least. He enjoyed milking the entire fuck out of each and every shift, there was never any sense of urgency on his behalf, and if there was a red light to hit, he'd tag that motherfucker! I was never working there with the intention of making this anything remotely close to a career, and with each passing day I was becoming further annoyed. My son was born in October of 2010 and I believe the store closed its doors in January of 2011, something close to that. I had quit prior to the store closing, but either way, I was pleased with the way things had unfolded. No more commutes, no more being trapped in a truck with long haul; that's what we called him because he loved long routes.

Any out of state deliveries and he was all over that shit! He'd say: "It's gonna be a long-haul tomorrow." Knowing I never had to hear that again or share a vehicle with him was a relief in itself, the thought of no more having to watch him swallow two gas station hot dogs before 7am every morning, and no more road trips to Nebraska, Iowa, and Kansas with that man brought me great peace.

My focus was once again on my child and I was having to re-acclimate to having one in diapers. Anthony was night and day from his sister. He wouldn't sleep through the night, had night tremors, curious about every damn thing, and loved to climb; for fuck's sake this was going to be a chore. At first it wasn't too difficult because he was still sleeping in our room, and during those months he'd sleep in his crib which was directly next to my side of the bed. When he'd wake up in the middle of the night for his feeding, I'd scoop him, roll over, hand him to his mother, and go back to sleep. He'd then feed, she'd hand him to me, and if he didn't need to be changed, I wrap him like a burrito and place him back in his crib. It was a well-oiled machine fully capable of operating in the dark. That was a humble brag because I believe all parents should take a moment to pat themselves on the back for enduring their children's bullshit. As months passed, he moved into his room downstairs, obviously this was our next challenge because nobody knows how one's baby is going to respond when they're placed in their own room after being sequestered next to you every night. It was about what we expected; he would cry and whine, but eventually fall asleep on his own, some nights were better than others, and he finally began to fall asleep without crying. That was merely one obstacle on this course because next, he realized he had long legs he could hoist over the top of his crib and pull himself out.

This was the moment we invested in a gate for the stairs, and also the moment his sister realized she was going to hate this phase just as much as us. Sierra's room was directly down the hall from Anthony's, so when he'd escape in the early morning hours, he'd go into her room, turn on the lights, and say: "Wake up sissy," which resulted in sissy waking us up, in order to tell us he was up. The worst part was how he'd smirk when we put him back in his crib. He'd be smirking through the side of his pacifier which meant he was going to escape again, and he thought this game of wake everyone up before dawn was highly amusing. This was when we actually installed the gate on the stairs in hopes of keeping little Jacques Cousteau contained. The gate was the first of a few failed child proofing experiments and worked well until he began treating it like his crib and repeatedly climbing over it. We had very narrow stairs and concluded it would obviously be better to leave the gate open or take it down so he wouldn't fall or trip while climbing over it; which negated the purpose of having a gate at all. Next came the child proof door handle contraptions, they were pretty much two pieces of plastic shaped to form around a doorknob. They snap and connect on allocated sides and allow for adults to squeeze and turn while twisting the knob. Because toddlers have smaller hands, they shouldn't be able to accomplish this, wrong! Anthony learned he could force his fingers inside the hole where they connect and smash his way into the pantry by forcing the two pieces apart, and after breaking two of them we cut our losses and accepted the humbling loss. Next contestant was the kitchen drawers, once his interest led to the kitchen, it was merely a matter of time before he began pulling out drawers, grabbing silverware, etc.

Our brilliant plan to address this was to buy the latches you install inside the drawer. Not exactly sure how it works off memory, but the quick version is you can pull the drawer a quarter of the way out, then it catches, and you have to apply enough downward pressure to continue accessing the drawer. Welp! Once again, my guy realized he could pull the drawer out with enough force to surpass the latch and gain access to whatever he desired. That would be strike three for us in the child proofing department and was now Anthony three, parents zero.

We now move from child proofing, and into the night tremors. These inconsiderate fucks mimicked a nightmare. Obnoxiously loud screaming, refusal to open eyes, and inconsolable for various amounts of time. In our situation, the time would range from five to fifteen minutes of what you would have thought was someone being murdered. I mean holy shit! Imagine being in bed wanting to fall asleep but also actively trying not to because you know you're about to be rudely awakened by the ear-piercing screams of a sleepy toddler who refuses to respond to verbal commands. It was like sleeping on pins and needles waiting for the other shoe to drop. This is where grandparents came in handy. Mom and dad would drive up from Arkansas, meet us halfway at a previously agreed upon location, we'd then make the exchange, and be on our way back to the awaiting arms of peaceful nights of rest. I don't know what kind of fairy dust magic grandparents possess, nor do I care. However, whatever it is, I'm thankful for it because once he came home, he had more of a calm to him. Who knows, maybe he just needed a break from us? Whatever the case, it felt like we had hit the reset button and had somewhat of a fresh start.

By the time Shannon had returned to work, we once again had things regarding the children up and running. Sierra was at school by 8am and I was back home within minutes adhering to Anthony's schedule. As familiar as I was with this, I was not liking the familiarity of being home while others around me seemed to be pursuing or living their careers. I was watching classmates from the academy get hired at the same departments I applied with, I was watching and hearing those closest to me go to work every day, come home with stories about co-workers, Christmas parties, and work events while I was struggling to even make friends. Making friends wasn't a luxury I was afforded at that time due to the limited access I had to actual time. On top of dad duties, I also had uncle duties. My sister and brother-in-law lived five minutes away, were active members of the world's workforce, and obligated to punch a time clock every morning, which meant I got to spend more time with my nieces. I'd be lying if I didn't say there were times I felt like nothing more than a glorified babysitter, but I also felt pretty accomplished at times. There were days when I had a car seat in each hand, and the two oldest walking single file in front of me. I was taking kids to appointments, doing drop offs, pick up's, dinners and bedtime. I was also making memories and bonding with my nieces, so it wasn't all bad. Plus, the bond the four of them share today makes it all worth it.

While doing this, I was still dealing with other issues such as my Crohn's Disease. It would flare at random times and have me wanting to tap out. I recall mornings Sierra would ask if I was okay because she'd notice me clutching or jabbing my elbow into my side to help the pain subside. I'd fake a smile, say yes and carry on. I clearly wasn't okay and was now dealing with the result of neglecting my health and Dr.'s recommendations for surgery. There was no way I could afford to be out of commission when so many people were counting on me to play my role. I also wasn't fond of the idea because statistics showed people with Crohn's have a higher chance at not recovering properly. Hence causing more issues post operation and possibly in some instances, more surgeries. That's all fine and what not, but when you're dealing with intestines and discussing removal, there is only so much intestine you can remove before you begin to run out of real estate. It was to a point where every two years around my birthday I'd be hospitalized with some form of complications from a Crohn's flare. I would try to postpone going in when I knew I was having a severe flare because I knew they'd admit me, and my birthday is the last week in December. I wasn't wanting to spend my birthday through New Year's in the hospital, so I'd hold off until the beginning of the year before I'd go in, get admitted, and they'd give me prednisone for my troubles. If you aren't familiar with this devil drug, allow me to explain. This lovely drug is a steroid that helps fight inflammation and does so very well. The only drawback is that it makes you an insatiable bottomless pit at times; at least in my case anyway. I don't know if it's the dosage or just the drug itself, but whatever it is, it always takes me back down three chins road, back to the days I had hot dogs for fingers. The hospital admissions and administering of prednisone may have fallen under operating procedure, but at this point they were merely serving as band aids on a bullet wound.

While dealing with that I was hoping to receive a call back for a testing date and had applications in with every department hiring in the area, both Kansas and Missouri. One day I received a call back from a department to come test and I still wasn't excited because I had tested with multiple departments and now understood this was just a formality. Nonetheless, I took the written and made it to an interview. They asked a plethora of textbook bullshit questions, followed by scenarios a five-year-old could find on a search engine. The others were things that could be answered in my resume and application had they actually read it. They asked me what I had done to prepare myself for a career in police work and I was thinking, ughh bitch, did you even look at my application, wait, scratch that question, can you read? If you could, you'd have the answers you seek. It felt like they had decided I wasn't a fit for their department prior to the interview and as if they all had somewhere else to be. The interview was them going through the motions and covering their bases so to speak. Hey, we interviewed our one colored person for the year so we're good, right? Two weeks go by and still no word from them. I would call and ask about my status only to get sent to voicemails or told the person I needed to speak to wasn't available. So, I did the next best thing, I went over their heads and called the Chief's office. His secretary probably wasn't too pleased with my dialect, but frankly I didn't give a fuck, and within fifteen minutes that dick hole of a sergeant I had been trying to contact for the past week called me back asking what it was he could do for me? I told him I had been calling to check the status of my application because I had never received a call or letter from the department. I gave him my information, he placed me on hold, came back and said: "I wouldn't hold my breath," then invited me to come in and speak to them about their decision. After recovering from the dismay brought on by his unsought choice of words, I definitely wanted a face to face with this douche canoe.

I wanted to see if his old gentrified ass would say that condescending bullshit to me when I'm sitting directly across from him, and to his credit, he did, his racist ass stood tall and I can respect that. He was just as much a bitch in person as he was on the phone. I can always respect someone for being who they really are. My wife and I were speaking our piece and explaining things from our perspective when we asked them to tell us how many white officers they had employed, they answered over one hundred. When I asked them how many black officers they had employed, they said three, and I knew for a fact that at the time, one of them was a school resource officer. So, in a city neighboring the urban areas of Kansas City, you have three black officers interacting with the public, hide one of them in a school, and you don't see a problem with that? His response was "we don't lower our standards to higher minorities." This bitch actually said that to me with a straight face. Lower your standards, you realize I've checked all boxes regarding standards to become a Police Officer in the state of Missouri, correct, exactly how would hiring me be lowering your standards? I don't even know what he meant by that response or how he felt the need to incorporate it into our conversation. So I took it as offensive, and as offensive as that was, it was also eye opening because I would never in life want to work for a department that has officers with that mindset, and before I said something to make the situation worse, we told them thanks for their time and left with the realization that these particular individuals have traded in their horse, bed sheets, and tiki torches for a badge. They could all eat a bag of dicks as far as I was concerned. This level of rejection in this particular arena was becoming more than unbearable, and the repetition of doors slamming in my face, being told I have no command presence, to go work at a park, don't hold your breath, and we don't lower our standards to higher minorities was comparable to a deafening and overwhelming feeling of failure.

Even still, my thought process was this is my last year of eligibility without having to go through the academy again so I should make the most of the time I have left, and decided to apply in Grand Prairie, TX, and Memphis, TN. I made it to backgrounds with Memphis until my background investigator called to notify me I was being taken out of consideration due to a gap in my employment history from the time my daughter was born till the current place in time. I explained I was terminated from my job, that my wife and I decided it would be financially beneficial for me to stay home with our daughter rather than get an under paying job where the little money I would make would go to childcare. I appealed their decision with a lengthy thought out letter written to the appeals board. Attached to the letter was a picture of my family. I'm guessing they just threw the picture away and never read the letter because I never heard back from them. I wasn't being dismissed from the process because I had a criminal background, or because something suspicious came up during the investigation. I was being passed on because I didn't work long enough, what the fuck kind of shit is that? It didn't seem like a legitimate reason to me, but hey, it is what it is, and the decision had been made. Once again, no dice.

On top of the rejection from these departments, it wasn't like my marriage was in the absolute best place either. It was showing cracks, but I did what most people do, ignored it and kept it moving. I wasn't at a place in my life where I was ready to have the conversation attached to those cracks, or deal with the fallout caused by aforementioned conversation. It had started a year or so after Anthony was born. Her 12-hour day shifts were causing her to miss out on a lot of the kids' lives. Not only that, it was putting a strain on us because there wasn't any time for us. When she would come home she'd be ready for bed because she was up and back at it by 5am the next morning, and for me, I was trying to do everything I could to free more time for the two of us once she got home. Have the kids in bed, bath water ready, and sometimes a glass of wine; anything I could do in hopes it would free time for her to sit and talk. It didn't work, it only helped her get in bed faster, which I'm not upset about, nor was I at the time. Slightly disappointed, but I understood completely. She was exhausted and literally didn't have the energy. It was shitty because I felt we were two ships passing in the night, heading the same direction for the time, but could easily break course at any moment.

We shared the same space, but nothing more. It wasn't a cold, dark, place, but it definitely wasn't in a warm, inviting, invade all my personal space place either; lukewarm at best. Due to how her work schedule conflicted with family, she decided it would be beneficial for her to switch to night shift in order to be around me and the kids on a more consistent basis. That decision showed me she apparently saw the cracks too, and this was her way of beginning to address them. I'm not saying that's what it was, but that's how I took it. During this time, we had also been discussing moving to California in order to provide our biracial children with a more diverse atmosphere. Not only our children, but me as well. I had been looking into academies in the San Diego area because I still had the desire to pursue it, and I figured I too would have a better chance in a more diverse environment. We then applied action to thoughts and began the process of looking for jobs and places to live.

Being a nurse, Shannon would obviously have no issue finding work, that was simply a process of seeing who was hiring. As for me, I was going to enroll in another academy and start the process all over, start fresh and move on with my life. I wanted to get as far away from Missouri as possible and wanted something for myself, something I could say I've earned, something that would not only provide me with income, but also a sense of financial stability, peace of mind, and a feeling of contribution. Something that would afford me the opportunity to leave the house daily, interact with adults and not just children all day, have a place to belong, possibly make new lifelong friends, etc. I felt I needed to do this for me. There had to be more to my life than being what I considered a glorified babysitter. Yes, I know you can't babysit your own damn kids, that's not what I'm meaning. I mean I was always the one taking care of all the kids while the other adults worked. It was more than redundant, I needed a change of pace, and once the research phase of moving was complete, it was time to set a date and execute our departure from misery.

○ ● ○ ○ ○

CHAPTER 4

GOING BACK TO CALI

In July of 2013 we sold all non-essential items, managed to fit the remainder into two trailers, and PRESTO CHANGE-O, there you have it, all done and ready to go. The drive actually wasn't that bad, there were two adults to each vehicle, and we drove in shifts or whenever the other was too tired to continue. Shannon said I had it easier because I was in my truck with my brother while she was stuck with the kids and Justin, which equated to her having three children and I none, which is exactly why I don't disagree with her. The kids did surprisingly well for only being six and two years of age. Justin kept their tablets charged and smooth sailing. The issues started to arise once we got to Phoenix. It had been a long day, we had gotten off course, rerouted through the mountains, we were all spent and on edge, and being in Phoenix in the middle of

July was only adding fuel to this inferno.

When we first arrived at the hotel, I thought we were just pulling over while we confirmed where we would be staying. The thought that this was where we would be staying the night never crossed my mind. The place looked like it was given a 2-star review and only because it was probably written by an employee's kid who was hard pressed for cash. At this point I'm asking Shannon what the fuck, while she's saying it looks nothing like the pictures online. She's upset, I'm pissed, Casey is agitated, Justin wanted to eat, and the kids wanted to get out of the car. Finding another hotel in such short notice would more than likely be a chore, and the way we were all feeling, it was best to suck it up and somehow make it work; which is exactly what we did, got checked in, showered, fed everyone and called it a night.

I didn't feel comfortable leaving the car and our belongings outside in that sketchy parking lot, so I slept in the car while they slept in the rooms. It didn't take long for me to regret that decision because even at midnight it was still in the triple digits, but what better way to cap off an already shitty day, right? I was more than ready to leave hell, and when the night sky conceded to the demon spawn sunrise, that's exactly what we did; ate, loaded up, made the six hour drive, and finally arrived in what would be our new home; San Diego, California.

Moving was supposed to provide not only some fresh air in the form of scenery, culture, and atmosphere, but also be somewhat of a fresh start for Shannon and me. Well, one out of two isn't bad and beggars can't be choosers because as we all know life has a way of reminding us we're only along for the ride, and our plans mean absolutely nothing. Unwilling participants in life's kidnapping scheme, we'll kick, we'll scream, and even cry at times, but our captor, life? It fails to give one iota of a fuck, and unlike the movies, the hits keep on coming.

Once we were moved in and settled, it wasn't long before my physical assessment test for the academy was set to take place. Upon successful completion I would continue to the written test phase and eventually onto orientation where those who passed were provided with facts, what to expect, and our financial obligation. Those obligations included but were not limited to: my uniform, gun, ammunition, extra mags, gun belt and accessories. Whereas, when I went through the academy in Missouri, I only had to pay the admission fee for school, and it covered my uniforms and duty belt. Weapons were provided by the academy when needed, and I was responsible for my boots and ammunition. Back here in California, I was also an out of state resident and didn't have the financial resources to afford the price of admission so soon after our move.

Prior to the move we had accounted for the out of state residency obligation, but the information received at orientation about the other financial responsibilities wasn't made available until the day of. So, due to unforeseen events and poor planning on my end, it was back to the norm, which equated to dad life for me. It was back to apparently doing the only thing I could do, or at least it seemed that way. Seemed like parenting was the only thing I was good at or was going to be able to do for the foreseeable future. Seemed like every time I made plans for my own personal life, something got in the way, interfered, didn't pan out, fell through, etc. Groundhog Day again, back at home and it couldn't have come at a worse time. We were in the middle of potty training and this time around wouldn't be like the first. I'm not going to waste time going over every method we tried because none of them worked. He absolutely refused to use the restroom and instead preferred the hide in the corner method. This was absolutely annoying because his bedroom was directly across the hall from the restroom, yet he'd rather go in his room than the bathroom, which is right there, the same distance! Trying to understand it only further upset me and I had had enough of this shit, literally. One weekend I decided this was it, this will be the weekend we make potty training our bitch. Put him in his onesie, left it unsnapped, threw him in a pull-up, and had a positive attitude. That last part lasted a few hours before I was ready to fight this kid. He would tell me he needed to use the restroom and would have no problem displaying proper use of the ONE technique.

However, when it came for technique TWO, he absolutely refused to sit and shit. He'd look around, go through the motions, swing his feet, put on some theatrics, flash a smile and say he was done. Then I'd have to pretend I'm happy he tried and get him down; all while knowing I'm not happy, and he still needs to use the restroom. This was becoming the trend for the day and the whole "make potty training our bitch" wasn't working out so well. Shannon was at work this particular night, and I had told Sierra I was going to take a shower. I told her I'd be out shortly and if she needed me for anything to just knock on the door. I also emphasized to only knock if it was an emergency because I just needed ten minutes to myself. I was three minutes into my shower before Sierra was banging on the bedroom door screaming dad and emergency. I come out of the bedroom soaking wet in a towel to see my son standing in the dining room by the table holding his pull-up. He had taken his pull-up off because he wasn't particularly fond of the way it felt after using it as a toilet, and in order to rid himself of that feeling he understood he could unstrap the pull-up and no longer have the discomfort his unwanted occupant provided. Took it off in the middle of the dining room leaving its contents on the floor.

Not only that, he decided he'd pee everywhere for good measure. Sierra was right, this was definitely an emergency. I snatched his ass forthwith and planted him on that toilet, I told him to sit there and shit! Do not move from this spot until you put something in that toilet. I was finished doing this dance and the power struggle was ending that night! Two minutes later he said he was done, I told him he better not be lying. I walked over and sure enough, he was done. Sierra and I threw a mini party, hugged him, told him we were proud of him, rewarded him with marshmallows, and called his mom.

That was the last night we ever had issues with him using the bathroom, and I like to tell people I literally scared the shit out of him. Anthony completing this hurdle was a big milestone for sure, but it was merely one battle won in an ongoing war. At this particular place in time I was having what I would consider major issues with my Crohn's Disease. The pain was intense enough that the hospital stays were once again a reoccurring thing. That inevitable moment I had been running from the last few years had finally tackled me; the years of saying I'll do it later, or I'll eventually get around to it were over. This surgery was happening, and I had no choice but to wrap my head around it.

The day Shannon found the correct surgeon was memorable because I swore up and down I wasn't going to like him. I was already pissed about having to have surgery, had thought of every possible way it could and more than likely would go wrong, and in my mind, nobody was going to be the correct surgeon, especially after our meeting with the first contestant. The problem with this recommendation was that he was a general surgeon and I was needing more of a specialty surgeon. However, he was covered under insurance and I needed surgery, so the very least we could do was hear his pitch on how he'd like to proceed. We met, and his plan was to drive home how bad my case was and continually reiterate the need to cut right away. However, he had no answers to the questions regarding technique, procedure, recovery time, successful surgeries, and seemed to be upset with me for asking questions. I know he's the surgeon and I should defer to his knowledge on the subject matter, but I didn't feel the answers he was giving, or better yet failing to give were adequate enough for me to do so. He wasn't happy when we left but I didn't care, the man was a dick hole and would've made Swiss cheese of my insides.

Next was contestant number two; this surgeon was out of network for insurance but was actually a specialty surgeon, and after that first in network fiasco, we had to try something. Day arrives when we're scheduled to meet, we walk into the waiting room and I had already made up my mind this wasn't going to be the right surgeon. While waiting, I saw this physician open the door to call his next patient. He was a small in stature man with an infectious smile and inviting presence. There were two surgeons that occupied offices at that location and since my wife had to do everything for me because I wanted to behave like a child, I didn't know what the surgeon looked like. Quick lesson for the slower ones, don't be like me, grow up. Once he had called his patient back, I told Shannon I hoped he wasn't my surgeon. Despite all the vibes I felt when I saw him, I was hell bent on being a douche about this. She obviously knew he was who we were there to meet with, but she wanted to get the full experience of this blowing up in my face and remained quiet. Moments later he comes back out, calls me back, and I look at Shannon like you motherfucker, you knew! She's smiling and smirking as we stand to walk back. We get in the back and immediately hit it off, one of those situations where everything just felt right. Put my mind at total ease and scheduled me that day. I scheduled the surgery for April 1, 2014, because I figured it was fitting how I had fooled myself into thinking I could continue to put something so pressing on the back burner and not have to atone for my decision at some point in the very near future. Ignorance wasn't necessarily bliss, but it was definitely enabling. The morning of the surgery arrived, and I was nervous, borderline nauseous. I have had surgery before, but never one of this magnitude. They were doing a colon resection, so you have to forgive me if I was a bit concerned about the thought of shit going wrong; pun intended.

Once inside the operating room, I vaguely recall a brief conversation with the anesthesiologist prior to waking up in recovery. The surgery was supposed to be non-invasive but took a hard left once he made the initial incision and saw the disaster inside. At that point he had no point he had no other choice but to resort to invasive measures and ended up removing over a foot of my bowel. Things were worse than he had thought prior to starting, which translated to my recovery becoming the worst-case scenario I had already envisioned.

Once out of recovery and back in my room, my surgeon came in and brought us up to speed. He said I had one of the worst cases he had ever seen for someone my age, my case was worse than one of his elderly patients, and due to the surgery being invasive I was obviously looking at a longer recovery period. Aside from that he said he had no other concerns, wanted me up and walking, they'd continue to monitor me, and he'd be back the following morning to make his rounds. That whole up and walking part was some bullshit. I could hardly even lay down without the use of drugs, and I literally mean that. When I came out of recovery, I kept telling them my back hurt and I couldn't fully lay down. When they took me down for scans, they had to administer a bolus on top of the pain drip just so I could lay flat for the scan. That compounded by the fact I felt like death and had zero motivation meant there would be no walking over here, I wasn't even walking to the bathroom and he wanted me to walk the halls. I get it, but nope, wasn't happening. Next morning arrives and when he comes in, I look just as bad as I did the night before. I wasn't feeling better, was hungry, couldn't eat, still in a lot of pain, couldn't get comfortable even on a pain drip, and later that evening I began to spike a fever. This fever persisted for two days while they tried their best to figure out what was causing it.

Hospitals are already the worst place to rest and every time I'd fall asleep, a nurse would come in for rounds, a medical assistant for vitals, or a lab tech for more blood draws. A revolving door of nurses, physicians, lab techs, and even nursing students. One day they asked if I would mind if one of their students sat in on my case. I figured why not, maybe she'll learn something. So, there I am like an extra on a doctor show, here is patient J, he's three days post op from a bowel resection, presenting with blah, blah, blah, not responding to a, b, or c antibiotics, we've hung this, administered that, he's not getting any better, and both his pain and temperament are borderline stable for the moment. I'm in the bed like yup, now one of you run along and figure out what these physicians can't. Day three and I'm now meeting with the infectious disease doctor because the general physicians have exhausted all options as to what they could possibly be dealing with that was causing me to spike 103 degree fever every day at the same time. They took cultures and finally discovered I had contracted VRE, which stands for vancomycin-resistant enterococci; a bacterial infection immune to most antibiotics, and it had formed inside my surgical incision. Once discovered they started treating me like patient zero because hospital policy said all personnel that came into the room had to gown and mask and that shit got annoying, fast! Once the correct antibiotics were administered, I definitely didn't feel like myself, but I did begin to feel like I didn't have one foot in the literal grave.

For three days that fever kicked my ass, and day two I was thinking great, perfect, out fucking standing, this would happen to me. I was laying there thinking why fight this. Why even deal with any of this shit? I didn't have the energy to sit up in the bed, let alone fight. The pain I was in felt unbearable at times, I'd say the pain mentally was definitely worse than the physical pain.

I could press a button and the Dilaudid drip would handle the physical for the most part. Between my ears though? If pain were measured in decibels, my mind would've been comparable to a squadron of fighter jets simultaneously breaking the sound barrier. I had told myself this was what I deserved for all the bad shit I'd done in my life, for all the times I've hurt the people closest to me, this was my day of reckoning, and whatever was about to happen, so be it, I wasn't going to fight it. That thought process changed on day four when my kids came to visit. They had come and seen me prior but Shann had kept them away once the fever started. I didn't want to comply with nurses, didn't care for the doctors, had mentally checked out, and I was being pretty short with any and everyone. I was definitely in a fuck off mindset and whatever happens, happens mood. Not exactly the ray of sunshine and positivity you want around your children. As I was saying, day four arrived, and in walked my dependents. They really had no clue as to what I'd been dealing with the last few days and were just happy to see me. That was apparently the jolt I needed because I started to tell myself it wasn't fair for me to quit on them without trying. I couldn't tell them to always put forth effort in life and then just lay there when it's time for me to walk my talk. I began to get out of bed and attempt to do my daily walks along the hallway. I asked to be taken off of my Dilaudid drip and administered oral pills instead. I also began to feel a little better mentally, not much, but I definitely wasn't on the same level of funk I had been on. I was just still very weak from the previous three days and the new antibiotics were working but they had quite a bit of ground to make up, but now that the infection had been addressed, and I was taking the necessary strides to satisfy the doctor, I just wanted to put all of this behind me, go home and get some actual rest.

That was my only goal, just get home so I could sleep without being awakened every few hours. A few days later I was able to be released from the hospital and I wouldn't say my doctor was thrilled about it, but he was meeting me halfway. I had been there a little over a week and was more than ready to go home. He sent me home with rules and pain meds, told me to rest and take it easy, and he'd see me at my follow up in a week. When I was discharged, I was sent home with what looked like pills you'd give animals and instructed to take them for two weeks. These horse pill antibiotics would continue fighting the infection and were a small price to pay in order to go home, so onward and upward it was. Getting home was the beginning of a long road back. Keep in mind I was hardly eating during this ordeal, hell, even weeks prior to the surgery I really hadn't been eating much. I was such a nervous wreck that food didn't appease me, not even a little.

When I went into surgery, I was around 265 pounds, and when I came home from surgery, I was around 245 pounds. That's give or take but you can form the picture, I had lost a pretty good amount of weight in a short period of time, mostly muscle mass, was very frail looking, and felt as bad as I looked. I also had this drain attached and partially sewn into my skin in order to drain fluid from the incision site. It would drain into a bulb attached at the bottom end of the tube, and prevented me from walking upright, which made my daily walks around the neighborhood a bit more challenging. I was wanting to get back on my feet, but it wasn't feeling like my body was on the same page. Nothing about my recovery was feeling right, and each follow up there was little to no progression with my incision site. They had removed the drain on my third follow up leaving me with just a small opening, but it wasn't closing or healing how we would have liked.

It was more so oozing rather than draining, and they couldn't figure out why. This led to more CT's and MRI's which discovered I had developed a fistula and it was going to require a second surgery in order to rectify this wrong. Nothing was going right and everything I feared prior to the surgery was unfolding. After my scans, I was laying on the table crying and the tech was this calming, reassuring voice saying things would eventually turn around for me, reminded me this was a minor setback, and things like this happen. It didn't make me feel any better at the time, but I knew she was right. I was just tired of life's shit and ready to be on the other end of things for once. I had now been dealing with this for seven months and was scheduled for a second surgery in December of 2015, two surgeries in eight months. That year could eat a bag of dicks for all I cared, funny saying that in 2020, but I digress.

Outside of my bubble of bullshit, life was still unfolding, and things still had to get done. We were moving from San Diego to Temecula, preparing for a second surgery, and attempting to be better mentally prepared for my second encounter with the scalpel. One of the ways we better prepared was by sending the kids to their grandparents in Arkansas while we cleaned and readied the apartment for the movers; yes, movers. After our move to California from Missouri, we decided we were doing as minimal as possible this time. That and the fact that I was still having active health complications, told not to overexert myself, and keep the lifting to under ten pounds. Why would I defy my doctor's orders? I mean, I was trying to heal, remember? Plus, moving fucks with your headspace and I needed all the clarity I could get up there.

Other than moving in the middle of July and my truck deciding to die on the freeway, I'd say the move went pretty smooth. We finally got settled in our new place, kids were home, and school had begun. Things were as close to normal as they could be for us and we had just crossed another item off of our list of things to do that year. Next was finishing preparations for surgery in December, setting up childcare, arranging work schedules, and flying grandparents out. This surgery was taking up more time and effort in our lives than it needed to be.

When the day of my second surgery arrived, I woke up that morning with a sense of calm I didn't possess the first time around. I wasn't this anxious nervous wreck. I was just ready to arrive, check in, and get started. Before they sedated me, one of the nurses was telling me I had beautiful children and how gorgeous my daughter was. I laughed because I was playfully thinking, here I am undergoing surgery and this woman is talking about my damn kids, this was about me! Maybe you could throw some encouraging you can do this, it's all going to be okay, don't worry type words my way, no? Thing is, she did exactly that by reminding me why I needed to have this surgery and get back to my normal self. The surgery went very well this time, but as I expected, the pain was pretty intense. When going to my room from recovery, I kept saying it hurts, this hurts, it hurts really bad, this fucking hurts! My pain was falling on deaf ears and my wife and doctor were laughing at the vocalization of my severe discomfort. They said something along the lines of they knew, it would be okay, and that's normal. Well, excuse the fuck out of me for being the only one out of the medical loop here; and furthermore, if this is normal, then fuck NORMAL because this hurts!

When we arrived in the room, my doctor regulated my pain levels and explained his process during the procedure, said it went extremely well, the fistula had been repaired, and he expected no further issues. This was music to my ears because his voice lacked the unsureness that was present after the first debacle, or maybe it was just the drugs, either way it was over. I was finally on my way to being finished with that phase of my life, and this time around I would only be entertaining hospital staff for two days before being discharged on day three.

When I got home it would be months before I was fully healed and recovered from the surgery. Although I felt better, I was still pretty weak, and eager to begin rebuilding some of the muscle I had lost. Around March of 2015 I had finally begun feeling and looking like my normal self. I had regained the weight back and didn't look as frail as I had months prior. I was back to my normal routine of dad, and though familiar and redundant, it was nice for things to be back to somewhat normal. The last few months had been hard on us all and I had grown exhausted of being the reason everyone was putting their lives and schedules on hold. I was ready to be a father to my children whom I felt I had mentally checked out on over the last few months. I was ready to feel like more of a contributor and less of a burden, and I was definitely more than ready for some structure.

○ ● ○ ○ ○

CHAPTER 5

REALIZATION

The one thing I did have plenty of time to do during that previous phase was think. Most of my time post operation was spent inside my mind trying to figure out who and what I am. The way I saw it, I had just undergone this process of repairing an imperfection, blemish, problem, while at the same time going through this grueling life changing obstacle course. Though the course may have been figurative, the pain sustained while enduring was definitely real. I was on some next level thinking and it wasn't going to stop there, that was simply the thought that initiated the avalanche of self-assessment. Assessment of foods I ate that possibly caused or contributed to the surgery, the medicines I was or wasn't taking, the approach I had taken to my diagnoses, and my childish, cavalier attitude regarding my health. I had to take a different approach and change some things about the way I was doing life. Not only did I have to make better life choices, I had to follow through and stick with those choices or risk being reacquainted with the scalpel.

Outside my fog of thoughts, reality was still very much happening. Sierra was getting ready for her first real competitive year of soccer while Anthony was preparing for transitional kindergarten. Because Anthony had been in daycare for years prior to kindergarten, unlike his sister, he had no problems acclimating to a classroom environment or other children. I actually think I was more upset than he ever was, and that was due to TK being only half day. I kind of get it, but you gotta understand, I was dropping him off like hey, here ya go, see ya when I see ya.

Not hey buddy, see you in exactly 4 and a half hours. Whatever though, beggars can't be choosers so I took what I could get. Now soccer? That was an experience. Sierra was towering over all of these girls, she hadn't really found her coordination yet, and this was her first time playing organized sports against legit competition. As a parent I was so ready for this. I was ready for her to begin experiencing all the things we've been telling her about sports up to that point. Excited to see her perform, score, play defense, all of it. I was a ball of emotions and couldn't wait to see how she did. I didn't know how good or bad her team would be, I didn't know if she'd get to play, and I was very much hoping it would be a great group of kids and parents that could all just get along, one happy soccer family with no bullshit is what I was aiming for. I aim high, I know, but I'd rather miss high than aim low.

The first year we got an okay team, didn't do great, but it was a great group and the established friendships are priceless. Second year she was on a pretty good squad, still hadn't fully grasped the game, but she was willing to learn, and enjoyed the challenge. Her third year was the year she began to come along because the team she was on had a coach from South America who really understood the fundamentals and inner workings of the sport. He and his wife's coaching helped Sierra grow exponentially in such a short period of time. She began learning how to use her body as a shield, stop and change direction gracefully, improved her defense, and learned how to properly kick. Whenever game day would come, it was "pass it to Sierra, Sierra inbound the ball, Sierra, take that shot!"

It was to the point she would be crying during and after games because she was exhausted. The dad in me wanted to take her home and get her off her feet, but the competitor in me was like aye, so the fuck what! Suck that shit up and embrace the suck, you were built for this baby, there's a reason they keep calling your name. That's how I coach my kids because quitting is easy, and nothing worth having comes easy, So FUCK THAT! That team won quite a bit of games that year but missed the championship by two games I believe. It was a great experience and we absolutely loved being a part of it, but I'm glad we enjoyed it because we weren't so fortunate come next season.

The following season we felt like the teams were unevenly stacked. Something that was known to happen from time to time, but whatever right? No! Not whatever, talk about shit end of the stick? Yea, that was us, and the real turd on top was this pushover coach who gave a D minus effort on a weekly basis and would always tell the girls it wasn't about winning. Um, then what in the fuck is it about, sir? It's 90 degrees at 10:00am on a Saturday and we're out here watching what resembles an execution. If it's not about winning it better be about competing at the very least. Shit, we're awake, we're out here sacrificing our skin to the sun, you better do something. One particular game we were losing but still not completely out of it, that was until dingbat Marty decided it would be a glorious idea to switch to a two-defender's mid field method. Mind you, prior to Sierra beginning soccer, I didn't pay much attention to it, so I was still learning quite a bit about the game. However, I know enough to know when your applied method isn't working.

I formed this conclusion when the other team's best and fastest player kept splitting our defenders to the tune of three goals in less than 3 minutes, at which point I literally yelled Oh c'mon, do something! Turd turned and responded, "It's okay." I almost lost my shit. I yelled back, "It's not okay! That's our problem, we lose every week." I had had it with that man. I was seeing my child cry after every game because they were getting their teeth kicked in week after week, and she wasn't understanding why her coach didn't care about winning. As bad as the season was, it did teach her a lot about perseverance and humility. Nobody wants to be on a losing team and at some point, it becomes harder and harder to keep showing up. She stayed with it though, and I believe she's better because of it.

The following two seasons were also disappointments in reference to equal competitiveness and coaching, but as I said before, such is life, it is what it is, and that didn't translate into the entire experience being a wash. We established a few genuine friendships and definitely made lasting memories, one of which would be me being ejected from a soccer game. I know you're all struggling to believe that innocent me was thrown out of a game, but it did in fact happen. I'll explain. Soccer Saturday, the day we get up at the ass crack of dawn in order to chauffeur our dependent to her team's demise. This particular Saturday the girls had an early game, and when we arrived the girls were warming up, parents were saying hello, exchanging pleasantries, setting up chairs, etc. Now, I don't know how many of you classify as soccer moms or how many of you know soccer moms, but if you're familiar with either of the aforementioned then you know they're some of the loudest fans in sports, and possibly even louder than the men.

These women get into their soccer. Some

games I've seen mothers yelling the way you yell at your television while watching a game. They'd be yelling and commenting on the game, and the referees never gave them a second look, as a matter of fact, sometimes they just smiled and continued officiating the game. I quickly realized I wasn't afforded that same luxury. The game was just beginning, and I mean literally just had kick off. I'm finishing saying hello, setting up my chair, go to sit down, see the field and notice the player was offsides. In a normal non-threatening way, I began to sit down, turn to my wife and one of the other mothers and said she's offsides, that's offsides. Next thing I know I hear a whistle, the referee is pointing at me and saying you're gone. What, excuse me? No, I'm definitely not leaving, I just sat down, I literally just got here and did nothing. What do you mean I have to leave? I tell him I'm not going anywhere but he was free to stand there as long as he wanted. He then picks up the ball and stops play until I leave.

Absolutely refusing to start play until I leave the

field because I said it was offsides. I hadn't said anything more than what other parents say on a weekly basis and I was being asked to leave. When he picked up the ball and stared me down it felt like he was making it personal and I couldn't understand why. I was very conscious of my surroundings, location, and environment. I was aware kids were around, my kids at that, and one of them was crying. Hence the reason I walked to the car and let it be. I was so upset and enraged; I had a million thoughts racing through my head at that moment. Here we go again with this bullshit. Look at this douche canoe singling you out in front of all these people. The mother next to you says way worse on a weekly basis, I've seen and heard one give the officials her opinion in a not so respectful manner, and yet I'm being asked to leave because I said offsides??

This shit will never end will it? When I was younger, my voice was always too loud, I was told to be quiet because other people couldn't hear over my voice. Literally brooding as I'm staring at this man. The incident ended with me leaving and the official apologizing afterwards. Was what it was, a learning experience to say the least, but at the moment there was a part of me that definitely wanted to fail that test. I really wanted to take that a different direction, but cooler heads prevailed and the adult in me showed up. So, let's raise a glass for growth, and toast it for keeping my ass out of jail.

Back in my mind I'm still trying to figure out exactly what it is I'm supposed to be doing with life. I knew I wanted more out of it than being a father and a soccer dad. Don't get me wrong, I'm blessed and fortunate to have the opportunity to be able to hold those titles but at the same time, I'm trying to leave my personal impression in this one life I've been given; so excuse me for wanting to shine and flex on people from time to time. Can I live? With that said, it was more tinkering and figuring shit out, leading me to realize I had some underlying issues stemming from childhood. My dad and I didn't have the best relationship growing up. Caveat, he didn't beat or abuse us, so scrap that, but he was very hard pressed on education, church, and respect. If I was placing them in order it would be God, respect, education. He was stern on us, but tougher on me. I won't lie and say most of it wasn't warranted, but even still, getting in trouble for not knowing what tools did what seemed completely odd to nine-year-old me. I don't think he fully realized the stress I was under trying to get everything right and live up to his standards. Being an adult and now a father myself, I understand some things and now have better perspective as to why he was the way he was.

A little communication would have been welcomed, but that was neither a focal nor strong point of his generation; hard work was which is why he didn't talk much but was always busy doing something. He led by example, and fortunate for him you don't have to speak in order for others to understand. That was cool and all, but little Jason wasn't about any of that. What he was about was riding his bike anywhere it would take him, catching lizards, playing in the dirt, playing basketball, and breaking ankles in freeze tag. I'm guessing you can imagine how this conflicted with church. In my eyes, any and everything fun was ruined by church. As many times as I had been and heard the same story told different ways by different people, I had formed the conclusion that church could be wherever three or more people are gathered. I mean, if I read and heard correctly. So why in God's good name do we have to go to a building every Sunday, listen to shit music, and smell old lady perfume for two hours when four of us live under this roof? Can't we just gather round like we do when dad makes us pray? We'd been doing our own prayer circle for years, why did we have to attend a service with all these zealots? I was under the impression God was a generous and nice God, this feels like neither; furthermore, I could be defending my neighborhood freeze tag championship instead of being nailed to that cross, but call me Isaac because it was always a damn sacrifice.

As a child Sunday morning turned into concerts, and our house became Club Praise. Dad would put on vinyls, turn up his ten-inch subwoofers, and we'd all be awakened to sounds of gospel music, dad singing, and for yours truly, the occasional belt buckle. I had grown immune to his Sunday morning pre-game routine and would do my best to ignore him. I would always wonder how someone could be so happy to be purposely waking up this early on a weekend to attend church. When I hear service, I think funeral, which is exactly what all of this felt like for me. Anyway, he also had these leather belts with pretty good size belt buckles, like belts you'd see at a rodeo, and they hung in the hall closet outside of his room. The buckles would make this jingling sound whenever he'd grab them and whenever I'd hear it, I knew he was coming for me, and I'd sit up on the bed as if I had already been awake. He'd come in, see me sitting there, look at the clock, then look at me. I'm up, I'm awake. He'd close the door and I'd roll my eyes thinking this shit can't be normal; every Sunday with this shit.

One Sunday I had made up my mind Saturday night I wasn't going to church the next morning, it just wasn't going to happen. I was going to watch cartoons, King Arthur and the Knights of The Roundtable to be exact. I said FUCK THAT MUSIC, and that belt buckle. Sun comes up Sunday morning, Club Praise opens, I proceed to roll over and ignore it like I always do, ten minutes later, jingle jingle, man this is it, you're about to get fucked up and you chose this, so don't bitch out now. My door opens and dad tells me to get out of the bed and get ready. I told him no, I'm not going, and his response was, "You heard what I said," and closed the door. Yea, and you heard what I said, as I proceeded to emphatically mouth, I'm not going at a closed door. Twenty minutes later the garage door opens and I'm still in bed. He sticks his head in and said I'd better be at church before they got home. I'm still in the bed like well, you know that's not gonna happen, so I'll be ready for my ass whooping when you get back. Until then, close the door, have a great service, praise the Lord, okay, bye now.

Hell no I didn't say any of that. I was thinking it while we were having our staring contest. He closes my door, I hear him start the van, followed by the garage door closing. At this point I'm beyond excited, I'm thinking hell yea, you just stood up to him and won that shit. Then almost immediately, I'm thinking nah bro, you didn't win shit but a free ass whooping, and it's coming in less than two hours, maybe a little longer if they catch the Holy Spirit at the end of service, but either way this won't end well for you. That was definitely one of those won the battle lost the war moments, and that moment of clarity was all I needed to get dressed and find a way to get to church before it ended. Church was about ten, maybe fifteen miles away on a bike give or take, which was almost perfect for me. Almost in the sense that I had a bike yes, but both tires were flat. It was okay though because if there was something I did know how to do, it was fix a flat tire.

However, because I was running on borrowed time and couldn't properly fix both flats I had to improvise. I realized they were both slow leaks and knew I only needed to go one way. I assumed I'd be okay if I rode fast enough, and with it being Sunday there wasn't going to be much traffic, which meant I shouldn't be sitting at too many red lights losing precious airtime. Only issue now was finding a pump. I ran down to my neighbor's house, asked if he had a pump, he proceeded to ask me why, I explained I didn't have time to get into it, but needed to put air in my tires so I could get to church. He was slightly baffled and probably thought I was on the path to priesthood with how bad I was trying to get to church. No brotha, nothing like that, I'm trying to survive, so if you could kindly give me the fucking pump, I'll be on my way. I get the tires filled, lock up the house, and haul ass down Miller St. in hopes of arriving to church in time.

The site of me flying down the street sweating, wearing dress shoes, and trying to keep my feet from slipping off the pedals while going as fast as possible on a bike that's consistently losing tire pressure must have been a site. Upon arrival I had worked up a pretty good sweat and both tires were completely flat. When I walked in, dad and I locked eyes and neither of us said a word. His eyes were saying: "That's what I thought," and mine were saying yea, whatever, I'm here aren't I? No ass whooping for me, so I won too, let's just call it a draw and get this torturous shit over with. Very long story short, we butted heads often to establish dominance and neither of us was willing to budge. I understand this was more than likely some form of normal behavior between father and son at some point of their relationship, but this went on until I was out of the house and then was always swept under the rug and never addressed. It never being addressed was some of the problems I was dealing with from my past, and me not addressing it with my father was keeping me from moving forward in life.

Coming to this realization led me to unload that weight in the form of words which turned into an eight-page dossier. If you're having trouble reading between the lines, I said I wrote my parents a lengthy, detailed, to the point, yet respectful letter emphasizing all the shit I needed to get off my chest regarding my youth and upbringing amongst other things.

CHAPTER 6

○ ○ ○ ○ ○

CERTIFIED MAIL

When composing the dossier, I didn't hesitate or hold back, it was just me, the keyboard and my thoughts. Hammering away, letting emotions come out in the form of letters, and because this letter was intended for the people responsible for giving me life, I was as respectful as possible, and gave it a few once overs to make sure it met appropriate guidelines prior to sending via certified mail. I sent it certified because I needed to know they received it, and since it originated from a source of love, I was allowed to be a little extra. Compound that with the fact I'm the youngest meant in situations such as that, it wasn't necessarily uncommon to find myself riding shotgun while entitled drove. Perks of being "the baby." There are very few situations where my entitlement completely takes center stage, but when it does it's always family related and I don't do much to stop it. I tell my siblings I'm the best because I'm last, and when you get things right, you stop, you guys weren't necessarily mistakes, but you were definitely practicing for the headliner, so make a hole, coming through. The letter touched on some things I'm sure they had no idea about; mostly because I wasn't much for speaking my mind back then unless it was in the form of shouting or crying, and also because controlling my emotions and communicating wasn't something I learned until later in life. Some of it was me seeking answers, other parts were me seeking closure. I was trying to move on but not without discovering some things and righting some wrongs. I also fully understood this was going to change the dynamics of our relationship, and I was here for it because up until that point it felt forced and weird, awkward church hug weird, and only with my dad, so yea, let's change all of these dynamics.

I spoke heavily on how he and I had never been on the same page because he was so dead set on trying to make sure I didn't turn out just like him when, NEWS FLASH, I was and am YOU! Everything I did reminded him of himself, and he couldn't stand it. It was like looking in a mirror and seeing himself as a child, all my nuances and idioms that mirrored his was a resounding reminder of something he just didn't like about himself. At least that's how I broke it down to him because from a child's point of view I wasn't understanding what in the fuck I did every day that upset him so much. To me it seemed like I was always in trouble, and to be fair, I wasn't, but the always ever so present tension made things seem like more of a powder keg than they may have been. I've always been a bit of an asshole and smart ass at times, but whatever, I got that shit from somewhere, correct? Maybe try a different approach, show me how to become the man you want me to be, talk to me about all these emotions, frustration, things I'm doing that bother you and let's fix this. Tell me what works, what doesn't work, what I need to scrap and what I should improve on, when to be serious, when to listen, etc. As inquisitive as I was, it was perfect timing to talk to me, however, being the non-talkative, strong silent type he was, that was all wishful thinking. I'm guessing this had something to do with the generational gap between us because figuratively there was a massive body of water separating our interests. Think more oceans and less lakes; he was more let's fish and cut wood, and I was more ride bikes and watch sports. He was all the way country, and I was Santa Barbara County black. Not Carlton Banks, but definitely not black ass Farmer John.

Fishing always took place on Saturday, which was the first indicator I was going to hate this. The drive was always fun or enjoyable, especially when he stopped for snacks, or when he'd let me drive on our way there. Other than that, pfft! We would drive about 45 minutes to a city named Guadalupe and park in this clearing surrounded by oversize trees that cast enormous shadows. We'd then begin our mile walk in soft sand while carrying his poles and tackle box to his little slice of heaven. When we'd get there, I'd fish for about thirty minutes, eat snacks, and then build sandcastles. I'd do this because the time I did spend fishing was never pleasant and my line would get tangled in the seaweed or with his because I was too close to him. I also don't have the patience to fish, so when I'm not catching anything, I'm struggling to understand the reasoning for staying out here with all this sand and water smelling like salted ass. It was hit or miss if he would get frustrated when having to stop fishing and come re-bait my line, and at first I would be worried he was going to be mad and get on to me for taking away from his fishing time, but then a part of me would smile because seeing him upset over the fact this could have been avoided had he left me to my own devices warmed my heart. Furthermore, I was also told I couldn't put on lotion because I'd repel the fish. If I could insert a GIF into this section, it would be a slight head tilt accompanied by a what in thee entire fuck expression. I won't even begin to act like I understood what that meant at the time, but this was my dad and I expected nothing less to come out of his mouth. Now picture me looking like a used chalkboard trying to figure out if brushing my teeth and washing my face was allowed. My belief was he just said shit like that instead of saying hurry up.

Really no sense in wearing lotion to go fishing is the way he was probably seeing it, and instead of interpreting it as such, he'd say crazy memorable shit like that. So, seeing him slightly agitated was a special kind of blessing, yes. Whatever though, let he who is without sin cast the first stone, right? Exactly, we all live in glass houses, so petty, set go, and I'm not even sorry. Needless to say, I don't think fishing ever went the way he thought it would, or who knows, maybe it did, but as far as me? Fuck fishing, bruh!

I also touched on how I felt like I was going through a rough time in my life with my marriage and needed to talk to my dad but felt I couldn't reach out because that part of our relationship was never established. I don't want to bash the man and act like he wasn't a great father in so many ways, but this was a son to father perspective and I needed him to understand I wanted to have an emotional bond with my father. I needed to feel extremely comfortable unloading my emotions and soul to him. I explained as a child I only wanted to feel connected to him. Everyone would tell me I was just like my dad and I hated it and them for saying it. In my mind I was thinking hell, you know more about him than me, so, whatever the fuck you say. I didn't want to feel that, I didn't want that to be the first emotion I felt when someone told me I'm just like my father. That's where we were though. I couldn't tell him hey, I'm on the verge of getting a divorce, me and Shannon aren't in the best space, shit was said, things were done and we had a come to Jesus moment, or that I had questions I wanted to ask regarding relationships. None of that was ever developed and I was wanting to make peace with it and move on. I wanted to tell him I had started taking photography classes and find out through him that he was once heavily interested in photography. You know, things that would've shown me I am just like him and maybe he's not so bad if we share so many similarities, just things that show a child they're not alone in this world and things that allow them to better understand themselves.

Information between dad and I was usually second hand, meaning I'd tell mom, she'd relay it to dad, and he'd call me to talk about it. Conversations were always awkward for the first few minutes until he'd get to the reason for calling. The feel of the conversation would eventually switch to tolerable but rarely ever enjoyable. The conversations always had an underlying feeling of awkwardness and seriousness. One of those situations where you were allowed in someone's home, but you couldn't sit on the furniture. It felt like we were both always waiting for the other to say something that was going to lead to "that talk," and since neither of us wanted to initiate conversation in the past, I felt now was as good of a time as any because we were planning our family trip to Cancun the following year, and who the fuck wants to be miserable in Cancun, Not I!

Because the letter was addressed to dad and mom, mom wasn't safe either. Again, caveat, it was respectfully written, and feelings were taken into account, but I'm handing out haymakers, and we're a few rounds in, can't stop now, right? I told her how I felt betrayed when she gave my shit away to some church troll cretin that convinced mom she needed it more than me. This pet of Lucifer crossed paths with us back in the late 80's early 90's, and the beast's name was Sister Henderson! I wrote that like I was saying Sasquatch. Please believe this extra-terrestrial WAS NOT my sister, that's just what they referred to everyone in church as, sister this, brother that. I had a few choice names for them as well but that's neither here nor there.

Back story, I had this pillow and blanket, an Afghan blanket with a pillow that was hand woven and given to me by a friend of my mother. I carried this blanket everywhere, covered up with it, laid on it while watching movies, whatever, it was my shit, right? Well, for reasons unknown to me, this witch had stayed at our house. I couldn't even tell you how she arrived, it's like she was just there, like the wind just blew her in on her broom. I have no recollection of her in my life other than this dreadfully unfortunate memory. She showed up, stayed the night, slept in my room, and decided she liked my pillow and blanket so much she just had to have them for her ride back to hell. For reasons I'll never understand, my mom gave them to her. When I say that shit hit different, I mean it left a proverbial bruise, so momma caught a haymaker too. I closed by telling them I appreciated and respected them for all they sacrificed for me, said I loved them, and in no way was I trying to beat them over the head for things I saw as shortcomings. None of those things translated to failing as parents, it was just me wanting to say the things younger me was always too afraid to say, and to please feel free to call me to discuss any rebuttal you may or may not have. If not, let's put it to rest and party it up in Mexico! Surprisingly, they didn't have much to say other than offer their apologies and promised to change some things. We spoke about it briefly and haven't touched on it much if at all since. Which I see as a good outcome because I feel all of our voices were heard, we each got to speak freely about situations, and I believe we all gained some clarity from it. It was also nice to feel like for the first time I was being allowed to see a softer side of my dad. I had mostly been exposed to the hardnosed, grittier side of James, and had grown accustomed to only that.

Seeing this softer, apologetic, humble side was weird as fuck, very weird. It was different seeing my dad make himself so vulnerable to me, and I wasn't quite sure how I felt about it when it was happening. I began to ask myself if this was what I was really wanting, was this the emotional availability I've been seeking from him for over thirty years? Yes, it was in fact just that, it was a moment I won't forget anytime soon, and it was the first time I had experienced it on that level. In my mind, I don't think that ever comes to fruition without the letter. Timing is everything and delivery is just as important, I feel I succeeded in successfully achieving both with that dossier, and now that I had achieved the answers I set out to find, it was time to follow through with closure, and turn the page on this chapter of my life.

○ ○ ○ ○ ○

CHAPTER 7

PASSPORTS REQUIRED

That was exactly what I did, moved forward and focused on this new relationship forming between my parents and me. Not only was this upcoming trip going to be my parents' first time out of the country, it was also going to be our first legit family vacation other than theme parks. See, we weren't that family taking exotic vacations or any vacations at all for that matter, no, we were the family that worked through summer or spent summer with extended family in Arkansas. Dad always preached family and taking care of each other, which meant the family superseded our childish needs for excitement in the form of copious amounts of candy, roller coasters, and a five-foot mouse. That was cool and all, but we weren't flying, we were driving. The road trips weren't necessarily the worst because we had one of those vans with reclining and turn around captain seats, pull down curtains, TV, VCR; I know, old right? A cooler, and a bench in the back that converted to a bed. If you had to take a trip halfway across the country, there were worse vehicles to do it in. This upcoming trip would be nothing like the trips of my youth, there would be no long-distance driving, and the hotel was all inclusive. A different vibe for a new beginning if you will, introducing mom and dad to the twenty-first century of vacationing, and they were more than ready. This wasn't a normal domestic in country vacation, this was passport's required type shit, so they were allowed to be excited about it, and they were, actually more excited than the kids, and that was okay because not only had they earned this vacation, they deserved this vacation.

For us, Mexico was about repairing old wounds, placing the past behind us, and creating new memories to build on going forward. The goals were to be around each other and things not be awkward, have conversations, be refreshingly open and honest about things, have no more tension, stay as cool as possible in that sun, and for the first time, have things seem easy and non-forced. Seeing the kids having so much fun made enduring the heat worth it, they couldn't have been happier, they wanted to order room service every night after being in the pool all day, and I was okay with it because I'd always order their nachos. The hotel staff would refill the refrigerator daily with drinks and snacks, but with the kids going between rooms we seemed to always be out of almost everything. Little vultures were having the time of their pillaging and plundering lives. "Uncle Jason, dad, we want to go to the pool!" Again? May I get drunk first, is that okay? How else does one expect to put up with underage terrorist that want to go on an all-day binge in the sun? I'm talking they didn't even want to hydrate, just go, go, go, and when they'd begin to feel the slightest hint of exhaustion, then they'd want to eat. They'd call time out, we'd feed them, and back into the pool they'd go. It was a win, win with them having a great time and the staff bringing drinks to the pool side; a family making new memories, and enjoying being in each other's presence.

As fun as the pool was, some of our fondest moments unfolded inside a variety of the hotel's fine dining establishments, establishments which offered a mass array of exquisite foods, including a Mexican restaurant that made these street tacos with limitless chips and guacamole, absolutely amazing. Next was this I want to say Brazilian restaurant. They featured a menu of pasta, chicken, steaks, and some stuff I can't pronounce, but again, all of it was absolutely delicious, yes, delicious, not good, but fucking delicious. So much so the hotel placed a limit on how many times you could dine there. I get it, but I would have definitely gone back repeatedly had they allowed it. Finally, they had this massive breakfast area that had everything you could imagine from waffles, to omelets, crepes, fruit, bacon, sausage, toast, hash browns, biscuits, etc. For me it was like walking into a candy store and not knowing where to start. I wanted it all because breakfast is my absolute favorite. I can eat it anytime of the day no questions asked, and I'll always be happy.

When I wasn't stuffing my face, or in the pool, I was walking around taking photos or looking at scenery. Prior to vacation, the thing I was most concerned with was taking photos. I was still fairly new with my camera, and I didn't want to miss the opportunity of being somewhere so beautiful with the right people and not properly capture the moment. I had planned on taking mostly candid shots, but also ended up taking an array of group photos that turned out not so perfect. I recall trying to get dad to take a picture with the grandkids and he's standing in the middle of the group looking like he just found out he's the father; it was laughable, but horrible, I told him to fix his face so we could get him and his fancy dress shoes out of the heat. It was hotter than satan's ass and there he was dressed for church on a beach in Mexico. When I tell you he's different, think extreme as possible, most of the stuff he says and does will surprise everyone other than those that know him.

Dad and I seemed to finally form a what's understood doesn't have to be spoken father son vibe. It had probably always been there, but he and I finally had an understanding which helped him realize it was okay to loosen the reigns. While in the pool with the kids we would swim over to a section that had an arched bridge walkway over top; it had this rather large wooden beam underneath and in between playing with the kids we would do pull ups on it. Something small, yes, but something we were not only doing together, but also enjoying, which was good enough for me. Mexico afforded me the opportunity to sit in the pool drinking with my parents while literally staring off into paradise. We sat there laughing because years ago none of us would've ever thought we'd be in that place at that moment. It was a simple moment of nostalgia for the three of us and having an actual candid photo of the moment makes it that much better. If I had done nothing else while there, I'm glad I did that. I'm extremely thankful I had that moment with both of my parents because as a child you rarely get to share moments with both parents simultaneously due to work, school, sports, and events amongst other things. So, to have them both there and to hear the three of us laughing without a care in the world was definitely a moment I'll never forget.

As fun as it was, it was time to head back to reality, and I believe I can speak for all of my family when I say we were ready to get home and out of the heat. Not that it wasn't warm back home, but not like it was there, the top of my head was peeling, and my black was cracking, over it.

CHAPTER 8

○ ● ○ ○ ○

TURBULENCE

It was nice to be home, and it wasn't until then that we realized just how much of a breath of fresh air vacation had been because four months into being back from Mexico, we were bracing to endure life's turbulence for the upcoming year.

In August of 2010, dad had double bypass heart surgery; after which he was in and out of the hospital for what seemed like any and everything. Complications from one medicine causing problems with another medicine, and at times it seemed like we were living in a revolving door. Months prior to Mexico he and mom had begun doing intense workouts with a family friend, they were both in the best shape of their lives and looked great, which is why I was slightly taken back by the news I was about to receive. I say slightly because I have this intuition when pertaining to my family, an intuition that affords me the luxury of knowing when something is off, sometimes I can pinpoint it, sometimes I can't. In this instance, I knew something was wrong, I just didn't know how severe that something was. Fast forward to a Thursday night in November and I had just sat down to watch TV when my phone rang. It was dad, but something about all of this FELT different. Whenever we speak, he always makes small talk for the first two to three minutes before getting to what it is he's wanting to say. This particular night he calls, begins making small talk and I interrupted him and asked what's up? I knew he had an appointment the week prior and I hadn't heard back from them until that night. His voice was somber, and I already knew the news wasn't good. He proceeded to say he had his appointment and his results returned positive for cancer.

I had a wave of emotions go through me at the moment, but from that point forward, I began mentally preparing for what was about to unfold. I proceeded to ask him what he wanted to do and where we all went from here? He didn't have all the answers, hell, none of us did. I just knew I was going to support whatever decision he made. I told him we didn't have to have it all figured out at that moment and we'd be there for him in every way possible. I assured him I fully understood he was physically carrying this cross on his own but we were walking right next to him; encouraging him when he wanted to quit, hydrating him when he needed fluids, lifting his spirits when he needed a laugh, or literally carrying him cause he couldn't stand. Whatever we could do to fight with him, we were going to do it.

It was now the second week in December, and I was preparing to fly in and help in any way I could. Dad was having some pain episodes and I knew it was getting harder for mom and my sisters to see him like that. He wasn't at a stage where he had lost a ton of weight. It was just at a point where seeing him holding back tears was gut wrenching because unless it was referencing his grandmother or the Holy Spirit, he wasn't crying, it just wasn't going to happen. I had also decided I needed to go because I could tell from my mom's voice that she was exhausted, she'd never admit it, and would rather fall flat on her face before asking for help, but I knew she needed me, and from the moment I arrived, I hit the ground running. Mom had me taking her to the grocery store at midnight and driving to appointments the next morning. With all the various ways I could lend actual physical help, I think I helped most by just being there because It felt like dad was trying to pick up where we left off in Mexico.

He was staying up late streaming movies and asking me if I wanted to start another series. One night he, mom, and myself were in their bedroom talking and I was sitting on the floor. When I went to stand up, he asked me where I was going? I said to bed, it's three in the morning, bro! He laughed and told me to go on then. Like I'm a bitch cause I can't stay up past three in the morning. I sat right back down in that floor, what you're not about to do is shoo me like a peasant cause you don't think I can't hang, nah buddy, fuck that, game on, let's stay awake, what we doing? Finally creating and having sentimental moments felt like me winning the lottery. While I was there not only would I would be celebrating Christmas, but also my birthday, New Year's Eve, and New Year; and with Shannon and the kids flying in on Christmas, I now had the opportunity to spend the holidays and birthday with family, a few clear skies during a storm never hurts, right?

The night of my birthday I ended up with our friends at their home until the early hours of the next morning. That night was great, alcohol was consumed, laughs were had, stories were shared, and memories were made. December 29 was a welcomed distraction from the reality that was forming around us and was also the night I remembered why I choose to refrain from consuming copious amounts of alcohol in one sitting. That night was enough alcohol for me in one trip, and I refrained from more than one glass of anything slightly resembling alcohol on New Year's Eve. Shannon and I stayed up with mom and dad while they watched the ball drop, and I'd say dad was enjoying himself the most. He was making himself margaritas and praising God for being alive to see another year.

Literally sitting on the couch kicking his feet like a child and shouting, all while pouring his margarita. It was actually quite comical, a character marching to the sound of his own beat. Though I knew why I was there, it felt like any other trip to my parent's home; it didn't feel like anything was different. That was until the time to fly home inched closer. The first time it got weird for me was when he began giving me his things. He gave me his Ray Ban Sunglasses he had since the eighties, his cold weather leather gloves, and his harmonica. Now that last one hit different because I have had my eye on that thing since I was a child. I would go into his room whenever they'd leave, get into his jewelry box and grab it. I can't play it for shit, but I enjoyed trying, so when he gave me that I didn't know how to feel. It felt like he was giving it to me because he knew he didn't have much time left. Which was weird, because to me he looked good, he had lost a little weight, but for the most part he still very much looked and acted like himself. His visual appearance didn't match his diagnoses and as awkward as that moment felt, it was about to be upstaged by our "goodbye".

When the time came for us to leave, we were loading the car and you could sense everyone was trying to avoid the moment. Shannon had given her hugs as fast as possible and ran off to the car, then the kids followed suit and left me hanging. I don't blame them because nobody likes goodbyes, and especially not in this instance. When my time came to say goodbye, I didn't want to go either. Dad was standing in the driveway seeing us off like he always did while mom was standing in the garage doorway watching. I had already said my goodbyes to mom and began to walk towards dad.

When I got to him, we both gave each other a hug and he told me he loved me, I told him I loved him too and I'd call him when I got to the airport. I wanted to say more but I didn't have the time, had too many thoughts going through my head, and I didn't know which to speak on first. The one thought I recall circling the most was me thinking that would be the last time I saw him. Up until the moment he gave me his things I had never processed it in that way, and his doing that was the moment it was solidified for me. I knew I had heard the words out of his mouth that Thursday night back in November, but that had only mentally prepared me; this was a physical preparation and I didn't like the way it made me feel. It was so much sadness so fast, and wanting to cry but at the same time not wanting to because introducing tears to this monstrosity would elevate it from sad to devastating, and in those moments I was perfectly okay with sadness because sometimes

the lesser of two evils is the only valuable
option.

○ ● ○ ○ ○

CHAPTER 9

HOLDING PATTERN

Returning home from that trip was bittersweet. It was nice to be back in my own home and in my own routine, but the situation we had left in Arkansas had us all in a holding pattern. Obviously when one gets a terminal diagnosis it's always a waiting game, but when one begins to give away lifelong possessions, you begin to somewhat wait for the other shoe to drop. It's a shitty and helpless feeling because we knew at some point his diagnoses would begin to severely alter not only his daily activities, but also his physical appearance. This began to develop in the months following our departure home and we were hearing from him less often. In this phase he was beginning to lose a little more weight and was definitely having more onsets of pain. From jump, dad had said no to both chemotherapy and hospice, so it was up to mom to manage his pain. Being a nurse for over 20 years this was nothing for her. She not only accepted the challenge, she welcomed it, and literally said: "I'm built for this," and built for it she was, handled it all with such grace, love, compassion, and most of all composure. The following months were up and down for dad, though he was dealing with all the pain, he'd still have his days where he felt good enough to do yard work or wash and detail his truck. If he wasn't doing either of those, he would be working in his garden. He always had a garden, and I mean always. Every place we've ever lived, he's planted a garden. Even when we lived in these apartments that had a front porch, parking, and no back yard. If you were sitting on their front porch at the time, you'd be looking directly at a line of trees with single family homes directly behind them. That's it, fence lines, dirt, and trees.

So, imagine my surprise when one day sitting out front, dad walks out of the apartment with an oversize bowl in his hands. I'm thinking oh okay, he's going to throw it the dumpster. No, he walks into the tree line and comes out with the bowl full of squash, zucchini, and cucumbers. I'm sitting up in the chair thinking where in the FUCK did you get those vegetables, and how did you just go into the tree line and come out with food like that? He knew what he was doing, and he knew exactly how I was going to react when he walked out. He walked past me laughing saying: "Nah dude, I planted my garden back there," and proceeded to walk in the house. I'm looking like of course you did, of course you fucking did. A real flare for the theatrics, this guy.

Whenever I would call and check in, mom would either tell me he had a good day or that he had a not so good day. I tried not to call all the time because I didn't want to seem like a hovering vulture, but at the same time I wanted to know how he was doing. I was always, and still am the blunt, direct, and to the point one in the family. I don't care for hypotheticals or bullshit, give me facts and don't lie to me, let me process it how I will, and I'll deal with it accordingly. Dad knew this because this is how he is; imagine that, us being alike. Knowing this, he wouldn't call me anymore and I had to be the one to initiate contact. Mom is also very much aware of the fact she can't keep anything from me, and yet and still, bless her heart, she tries. Whenever we would speak, it was all the things she wasn't saying. She was saying a whole lot without touching on specifics. When I would call and catch him during the day, he would sound exhausted, I would ask mom why he sounded like that and it was always something along the lines of he may have over done it yesterday while washing the truck or doing yard work.

Okay, that made sense to me because he was always moving and never fond of sitting still. If he had energy to move, he was going to move. So, her explanations always made sense until he was still sounding like that without doing any physical exertion. I'd ask mom if he did anything the last few days and she'd tell me he got up, ate breakfast, sat on the couch, took a nap, and made it back to bed. Yet he was still sounding winded and at times whispering. I told Shannon I need to go back, and I have to see him for myself because everything I'm feeling is painting a grim picture. Feeling the way I felt, I called my brother-in-law to get his perspective of things, he lived there, saw him on a daily basis, and I knew he wouldn't sugar coat it when I asked him how dad looked. He told me dad didn't look good and, in his opinion, he wasn't doing as well as mom was portraying. She is our mother, and her job is to protect us, I get it. There isn't a book on when and when not to protect, so if she felt compelled to shield us from the eye of the storm for as long as possible, that was her right. However, being equipped with this newly obtained knowledge was all the confirmation I needed to get my ass back to Arkansas.

When I arrived, I walked into their bedroom to see dad lying in bed with his head propped up on his pillows. He had lost a good amount of weight, was very frail, didn't have much energy to speak, and when he did, it was barely a whisper. He smiled when I walked in, I gave him a hug, told him to get his rest, and we'd talk later. He didn't have to say a word for me to tell he was overly joyed, not only because of me, but because my brother had also flown in and both sisters were there as well. He now had all of us under the same roof.

This trip was obviously difficult for a few reasons. It wasn't necessarily difficult for me to see his physical decline; however, it was very difficult for me to stand by and watch him look out the window wishing he could be out in his garden. It hurt for me to be in the garage and see his fishing poles, car cleaning supplies, yard tools, etc. It hurt looking at them because I knew how badly he would give anything to be able to do the things he loved. Another reason it was difficult was because it was the first time I saw mom break down. I had just went to start the car and came back inside to tell them everything was ready whenever they were.

Mom said dad wasn't going to be joining, and that it would just be the two of us. I finished helping her in the car and when I went around to get in, she was crying. It was her first moment of not knowing what to do, he had wanted to go so bad but couldn't. She grabbed my hand and we just sat in the driveway having a moment. It was the first time where I felt I had to be strong for her. I had to allow her to have her moment before getting back in the fight. Seeing her like that made me feel an assortment of emotions, none of them good. It was the first time in my opinion that mom acknowledged the possibility of a future without dad. Maybe she had prepared for that months ago, I don't know, I'm saying she never portrayed any sign of doubt regarding his condition improving until that moment.

Since there wasn't much laughter involved during this phase, I figured I'd change that whenever I could. One morning while in an appointment, dad had mentally checked out and began staring out the window. The nurse continued talking and looking at him as if she was trying to figure out if he was paying attention to what she was saying. She paused and asked if he usually does this?

I said if you're referring to mentally checking out of a room when he's no longer interested, yes, he does that all the time. He looked over and smiled, and I asked if he wanted to leave, he nodded yes, I grabbed his wheelchair, thanked her for her time, and informed her we would be on our way. While pushing him down the hall I may have gone faster than required, but he was smiling so I didn't care, and at that point you definitely take what you can get. When we returned home, dad got back in bed and slept for most of the day. This was his new normal, he could hardly muster the energy to sit upright in bed, let alone get out of it. I can't imagine what he was feeling being able to see and hear us, but not interact. We would leave the bedroom door open so he could feel as close to us as physically possible. It was rough watching him trying to be so strong and hold on for us. It FUCKING SUCKED!

He wanted us to come gather around the bed and speak openly about our feelings toward the situation and told me to go first. I told him it didn't matter what we wanted, and us asking anything more of him at that point was selfish, you've been fighting, you've been holding on, and if you feel you're tired of fighting, you can let go, we'll be okay, we don't have a choice. Opinions obviously varied as we went around the room, but it felt as if he was gauging the temperature of the room in order to determine if it was okay to transition. A few days before I was set to fly home, dad had one of his "touch and go" stints. He was lying in bed and had dozed off into what seemed like death? I was standing at the foot of the bed watching mom go into full on nurse mode.

I watched her work. I was in awe looking at her and thinking, one, how much of a Kilimanjaro she had been through all of this, and two, this is what in sickness and in health, and for better or for worse looks like, this epitomizes love. These moments were obviously excruciating in more ways than one for dad, but as far as pain, mom was right there with him. Watching the man you've loved your entire adult life slowly transition away from you while trying to stay strong is a death all in its own. While he was enduring, mom began to pray, this was something she ALWAYS did, mom and dad both. Because dad had decided he didn't want hospice, nor any life saving measures administered when his time to expire arrived, all she could do was pray. She would also talk to him in attempts to guide him back to the sound of her voice. While talking to him she said: "We're okay, all we need is Tylenol and Jesus." I said yes, and we need to put that on a shirt! It was moments after that when dad gasped and came back, he had this look of why on his face, why did I come back? For me, that was the moment the other shoe finally dropped and very much solidified the beginning of the end. Watching him, that made it very difficult to fall asleep that night, and when I eventually momentarily slept, I woke up with anxiety and fear that he had passed while I was wrestling with my version of sleep. I remember thinking, I don't know how my mom does this, the stress accompanied by the plethora of emotions I was feeling must've been a million times worse for her, yet and still, she was ice water, and a calm amidst a storm.

When I walked into their bedroom the following morning, I did so in a hesitantly peeking kind of way, slowly walking in and seeing him sitting up in the bed; whew, a moment of relief! It was times like I learned to really take in and celebrate small victories. Another awakening and teachable moment created by this shit storm, but a moment of clarity can have lifetime effects, so, in this particular instance I'll take the good with the oh so obvious bad. That morning he wanted to get out of the bedroom and sit on the couch. He had a cane he could use for such occasions, but he would rather use it for firewood than use it as support. Though that may have been acceptable to dad, it was not acceptable to mom, nor any of his kids, and needless to say, he used the damn cane.

When he wanted to go back to the bedroom, he said he wanted to walk without his cane, I told him that was fine, but I was walking with him and it wasn't debatable. He made it to his bedroom door before his legs gave out, he said he was sorry his legs were so weak, and I said there was no need to apologize, I got you, we're almost there, and I bet you're glad I'm walking with you now. We both laughed and I helped him back to the bed.

Every day came with more anxiety, it was so much waiting around and feeling helpless. The morning of the day of my flight, I was sitting on the couch when dad called me. I momentarily sat there in disbelief because it sounded like my dad, not the whispering and winded version of himself that he had become over the last few months, but his actual normal self. He had his deep underlying tone back. I ran in there like YES, you called me? He asked me if I had eaten and if we left him anything? I smiled, laughed, said yes, and what do you think? Told him to get up and find out. He came out of the bedroom, asked mom for his coffee, and somewhat jokingly said. "It better be hot." If you could have heard the way I laughed. I thought man I don't know what this is, but this is definitely him, he obviously feels out fucking standing because he is most definitely in original form.

I loved it, it was perfect timing, it was exactly what we needed to see out of him; well, me anyway, and not that he hadn't been fighting, but he had been fighting so much that the energy exerted while fighting sequestered his personality. So, to see it come back taking center stage the way it did was nice. We were so caught up in the moment we failed to realize what was unfolding. When we were children, dad said when it was his time to expire, he wanted to have breakfast at home surrounded by loved ones. He woke up that morning, somehow felt like his normal self, mustered the energy to sit at the table, eat breakfast with his sons, and fulfill one of his lifelong wishes. The man was such an overachiever! The time was nearing for my evening flight home, obviously a moment I'd been dreading since arriving because I knew this one was different. I fully understood this trip wasn't going to be the same when it came time to say goodbye, and for days I had been wrestling with what I would say to him and still came up with nothing. I walked in as he sat propped up in bed, walked over to him, kissed the top of his head, told him he was doing great, and that I loved him. He smiled and whispered he loved me before I turned to head out.

○ ○ ○ ○ ○

CHAPTER 10

WHEELS DOWN

F rom the time I was wheels down in California there was an overwhelming sense of the final countdown commencing. None of us knew exactly how much sand was left in the proverbial hourglass, but it was clearly dissipating at an accelerated rate. I returned home September 10, and he passed away 4 days later.

The morning of his passing mom had sent a group text asking us to fast until 6pm that evening; why, I don't know, this was and still is normal behavior with my parents. When they're "moved by the spirit," we don't ask questions, we just ride the Holy Ghost train and let Jesus take the wheel. That evening, he passed away a little after 6pm and when they called to tell us, I was in the kitchen washing dishes. I recall finding it odd that at the moment of his passing

I was washing dishes; odd because in the days of my youth dad would always delegate me to wash dishes, and when I was finished he would inspect my work to make sure I didn't leave water spots or stains on anything. As much as I despised washing dishes as a child, it actually brings me peace as an adult, something I loathed so much in my adolescence has now become a thing that reminds me of my dad. It's crazy how he always had the last laugh, always! It's annoying how he did it, but his timing was always impeccable so it's only fitting he stayed true to himself until the end.

This time around things became a blur, I felt like I had flown back and forth so much in the last few months that things all ran together, and I had zero concept of time. Being there and seeing him at the funeral home was just another step in the closure process. I was staring at my deceased father wondering how we got here and how we continue living without him. He looked as good as one can for being deceased, but he had a look on his face that we all hadn't seen in quite some time; it was the look of peace. He wasn't full on smiling, but he definitely looked like he was finally resting. That made the blow land a little softer than it may have had that not been the case.

This new reality was pretty shitty, but once again, the way my mother handled herself during all of this, even through the service, was quite impressive. Though, when your spirit animal is Jesus, it provides full explanation as to how she was an absolute mountain and gold standard on composure. I would have liked to think I was near or on her level composure wise, but I knew I wasn't. I was okay with the fact that he was now at peace, yes, but I wasn't okay with the fact that I was just now getting to know, learn, and understand him. I wasn't okay. We were finally at a place in life where we could be friends as well as father and son and now he's gone, I was NOT okay with that.

I was now left dealing with not only the weight of that, but also the weight of what I was going to speak about at his service. I had a few stories in mind, but that wasn't my biggest issue. My concern was how was I going to handle it, would I be able to control my emotions well enough to speak about my late father, and would he be proud and approve of what I shared? I wanted to do him as much justice as possible and not fuck this up when things mattered the most. When I arrived at the church there were quite a few people already there. So much so, there was no parking and I had to drop mom and family off in front while I drove around to park. As I drove off, I thought well damn, we're kind of a big deal today and we can't even find parking, I mean fuck, the audacity! I laughed it off and finally found parking around the back in this empty section of the parking lot.

I pulled in and it was facing this beautiful glass display on the back end of the church wall. I sat there staring at it with a plethora of emotions coursing through me. A fuck ton of sadness compounded by anger and severe frustration.

I was a ticking time bomb and knew I had minimal time to figure my shit out. I achieved this by white knuckling the steering wheel, closing my eyes, deep breathing through my nose, and thinking how wrong it was that I was driving his truck to his funeral, how fast this day got here, I was thinking Cancun, him giving me all of his things. All these thoughts came rushing to the forefront of my mind like an avalanche. I opened my eyes, told myself to get out of the fucking truck, and place one foot in front of the other. That's exactly what I did until I took two steps and some gentleman smiled and casually asked how I was doing while smiling and walking off. I watched him walking off all while thinking it must be God because had you stayed for my reply you wouldn't have liked my answer. Now, let me follow that up by saying I know the man was just out of habit asking how I was doing, just making casual conversation, but that entitlement I mentioned earlier sometimes shows up at the worst possible moments, and in that specific moment I was along the thought process of bitch you should know who the fuck's funeral you're attending, and if you do in fact know, you know that he had four children and I'm one of them. Attention to detail matters to me, but this was nor the time, or the place to be concerned about semantics. The fact I was able to allow my mind to go there at that moment only confirmed I had exactly what I needed in order to compose my shit while speaking about the late homie.

When my turn came to speak there was a collective holding of breath by a few of those closest to me because they knew where my headspace was and there was no telling what could possibly come out of my mouth. I sat down on the front steps, opened my mouth, said a few words, cried for a minute or two, then began. To me it felt like five minutes when in reality it had been closer to fifteen, I remember being there and saying the words, but I was so in the moment that I struggle recalling bits and pieces of it.

For days leading up to and even after the

service, mom had been sharing some things with me about my dad. Stuff that could help me piece together and correlate things within my personal life. Things that would help me make sense of where something may necessarily stem from. Cause we all know as children, we don't always see every side of our parents, there are things every parent keeps from their children until they're ready for the truth, or possibly even never, who knows. Point is, he was no longer here for me to go directly to the source and I had a lot of questions. Mom and I spent those aforementioned days filling in the blanks and sharing stories. We laughed, we cried, we made sense of some things, and began living our new reality, a reality where dad was no longer physically with us. Just being in the house was extremely weird, it was difficult to see his things, smell his cologne, and not be able to see or hear him. I was ready to get the fuck out of there, I was partially trigged as my sister says, and I didn't want to be there any longer than I had to be, every little thing was reminding me of my dad.

The day we were leaving, my sister was picking weeds out of her yard and I was watching her thinking that's exactly how I look when I do that, that's dad coming out in us, I almost lost it, I was done. I told the kids to get their shit, give hugs, say your goodbyes and get in the fucking car. Returning home, I was an emotional mess, an unwilling participant on this rollercoaster of grief; and all this up and down bullshit had me ready to punt something or someone in frustration. I was trying to mow the lawn one morning and instead found myself throwing the attachment for the leaf blower. This grief was kicking my ass and there was nothing I could do other than allow it to run its course. I got to the point where I embraced it and if I felt it coming on, I'd let it happen. Figured it was easier than getting upset and adding another component to an already unstable composition. Sometimes the moments weren't that bad because they allowed me to connect some proverbial dots and make sense of things.

It's hard for me to say I feel closer to him in death than I ever did while he was living, but because I wear his jewelry and see his picture daily, this is how I feel. As a child he would tell me he'd rather beat my ass than let the police do it. Imagine seven-year-old me looking at him confused and wondering why the good guys, the guys that come to our schools and let us play with their sirens, why would they want to beat my ass? I thought he was talking nonsense, but here we are in 2020 and that statement makes all the sense in the world. He was saying that when I was seven and I understood none of that rhetoric until my adult life.

Hearing of the things he experienced as a child and having a better understanding of the man clearly validated why he was as hard on me as he was, and why what seemed like nitpicking to me was merely seen as teaching to him. He was so hard on me because he understood what it was like being a black man attempting to go through life in a world where we're not accepted. I wish he was here for me to tell him I understand now, I understand now that I've been pulled over because I fit the description of a jewelry store robbery, or I understand now why you pushed me to be better than the other kids. I get the fact that this world wasn't designed with us in mind and I have to work twice as hard to get half of what others have. I wish he was here for me to tell him I'm currently going through that with his grandson, and I wish he was here for me to tell him it's his fault I like westerns even though I hated them as a child. He would get up earlier than us on the weekends just to beat us to the remote. We wake up excited to watch cartoons only to see his ass watching "shoot em ups" as he referred to them. He got up earlier so he could watch fucking westerns! Now here I am as an adult watching my fair share of the exact same thing, and I'm sure he'd find that comical. Therefore, rather than referring to those moments as grief, I now categorize them as moments because I'm not grieving, I'm learning and developing. I've learned so much about myself with his passing and finally understanding if I want the results I seek, the results I envision, then I have to not only say things differently, but when the opportunities present themselves, I have to CHOOSE to respond differently. That small act alone is growth and stands as an accomplishment all by itself.

You'll hear people say live your life, or you only get one life. Sadly, most of us don't understand what they're meaning until we experience personal loss. Maybe that isn't the case for any of you, but for me, experiencing something definitely gives me a different perspective and feeling than I would have if I didn't experience it. Not once did I envision my adult life without my dad in it while I'm still in my thirties. That possibility never played out, yet here we are, me in my thirties and my father no longer with us. It's only helped me realize I don't have forever to make my dreams a reality, I'm closer to 50 than 20, and time waits for nobody.

Which led me to Milestone Margaritas, you can apply this term literally or figuratively; however you choose, if you're an overachiever, I'd recommend the latter in order to avoid alcoholism. It works like so, in everyone's life, at some point, they accomplish something, yet for reasons unknown, they fail to take the time to celebrate or acknowledge accomplishments that aren't deemed worthy when weighed on society's scales. So, instead of using their scales, I'm proposing you use your own. Remember the time you potty trained your demon spawn that was determined to never use the bathroom? Pour a glass! Used your words instead of ugly crying and screaming into a void? You guessed it, have a glass and bring the bottle. Got a promotion at work, out fucking standing, Milestone Margarita! Pour it up and celebrate you because if you don't, who will? Once again, not suggesting any of you go full on alcoholic, and milestones can be celebrated in many ways. The point I want you all to take away is this, learn to celebrate you and take full advantage of the opportunities you're presented with while you still can.

They say it takes a village to raise a child, well, I also believe it takes the correct village to do life with. Having the right people standing next to us during one of our most challenging moments made all the difference in the world. Their help and support could never be described in words, only with action, which is why I'm all for raising a glass and celebrating those who celebrate you, cheers!

ABOUT THE AUTHOR

A product of James from the 805 that over time grew into a conundrum inside an enigma who enjoys using words in order to accurately portray the thoughts encompassing my mind.

CPSIA information can be obtained
at www.ICGtesting.com
Printed in the USA
LVHW081209141220
674120LV00004B/10

9 781735 920337